Interpretation of Customary International Law

Brill Research Perspectives in International Legal Theory and Practice

Volumes published in this Brill Research Perspectives title are listed at *brill.com/rplts*

Interpretation of Customary International Law

Of Methods and Limits

By

Panos Merkouris

BRILL

LEIDEN | BOSTON

Funded by the European Union

European Research Council
Established by the European Commission

This contribution is based on research conducted in the context of the project 'The Rules of Interpretation of Customary International Law' ('TRICI-Law'). This project received funding from the European Research Council ('ERC') under the European Union's Horizon 2020 Research and Innovation Programme (Grant Agreement No. 759728).

Library of Congress Control Number: 2024946182

Typeface for the Latin, Greek, and Cyrillic scripts: "Brill". See and download: brill.com/brill-typeface.

ISBN 978-90-04-54415-4 (paperback)
ISBN 978-90-04-52999-1 (e-book)
DOI 10.1163/9789004529991

This book is printed on acid-free paper and produced in a sustainable manner.

Contents

Abbreviations

AIDI	Annuaire de l'Institut de Droit International
All ER	All England Law Reports
ARSIWA	Articles on the Responsibility of States for Internationally Wrongful Acts
Art/s	Article/s
Australian YBIL	Australian Yearbook of International Law
BerkJIntlL	Berkeley Journal of International Law
BYIL	British Yearbook of International Law
CAVV	Advisory Committee on Issues of Public International Law
Ch	Chapter
CIL	Customary International Law
CJEU	Court of Justice of the European Union
CUP	Cambridge University Press
Doc	Document
DSB	Dispute Settlement Body
DSU	Dispute Settlement Understanding
EC	European Communities
ECtHR	European Court of Human Rights
edn	edition
EJIL	European Journal of International Law
EU	European Union
EurJLegStud	European Journal of Legal Studies
EWCA	England and Wales Court of Appeal
EWHC	England and Wales High Court
FCAFC	Federal Court of Australia: Full Court
GC	Grand Chamber
GYIL	German Yearbook of International Law
IACtHR	Inter-American Court of Human Rights
ICC	International Criminal Court
ICJ	International Court of Justice
ICJ Rep	International Court of Justice Reports
ICLQ	International and Comparative Law Quarterly
ICSID	International Centre for Settlement of Investment Disputes
ICTY	International Criminal Tribunal for the former Yugoslavia
IHL	International Humanitarian Law
ILA	International Law Association
ILARC	International Law Association Conference Reports

ILC	International Law Commission
ILM	International Legal Materials
LGDJ	Librairie Générale de Droit et de Jurisprudence
LJIL	Leiden Journal of International Law
LoyLAInt'l&CompLRev	Loyola of Los Angeles International and Comparative Law Review
MichJIntlL	Michigan Journal of International Law
MichLRev	Michigan Law Review
MPEiPro	Max Planck Encyclopedia of International Procedural Law
MPEPIL	Max Planck Encyclopedia of Public International Law
MUP	Manchester University Press
NSWSC	New South Wales Supreme Court
NZSC	New Zealand Superannuation Cases
OUP	Oxford University Press
PCIJ	Permanent Court of International Justice
QB	Queen's Bench Reports
RdC	Recueil des Cours de l'Academie de Droit International de la Haye
rev	revision
RGDIP	Revue Générale de droit International Public
Sct	Section
UK	United Kingdom
UN	United Nations
UNCLOS	United Nations Convention on the Law of the Sea
UNRIAA	United Nations Reports of International Arbitral Awards
UNTS	United Nations Treaty Series
USA	United States of America
VCLT	Vienna Convention on the Law of Treaties
Vol	Volume
WLR	Weekly Law Reports
WTO	World Trade Organization
YBILC	Yearbook of the International Law Commission
ZaöRV	Zeitschrift für ausländisches öffentliches Recht und Völkerrecht

Interpretation of Customary International Law

Of Methods and Limits

Panos Merkouris

1 Introduction[1]

According to legend, once a rumour started that Mark Twain was gravely ill. So far did this rumour spread that an American newspaper, so the story goes, printed his obituary. When Twain was informed about this, he famously quipped that 'the reports of my death have been greatly exaggerated'. Similar reports have been made with respect to customary international law (CIL).[2] These as well have been greatly exaggerated.[3] CIL as one of the formal sources of international law is alive and well, so much so in fact that the International Law Commission (ILC) a few years ago revisited this source with the aim of clarifying the method of its identification. Somewhat unsurprisingly the ILC focused on the classical two-elements approach and its Final Outcome in the form of Draft Conclusions is heavily influenced by this choice.

A topic, however, that although not part of the official work of the ILC,[4] made its presence felt[5] is that of CIL interpretation. Despite the simplicity and obviousness of the idea, it has not been the object of in-depth study, at least not

---

1 This contribution is based on research conducted in the context of the project 'The Rules of Interpretation of Customary International Law' ('TRICI-Law'). This project received funding from the European Research Council ('ERC') under the European Union's Horizon 2020 Research and Innovation Programme (Grant Agreement No. 759728). The sources mentioned in the current study are up to date at the moment of writing, ie November 2022.

2 JP Trachtman, 'The Growing Obsolescence of Customary International Law' in CA Bradley (ed), *Custom's Future: International Law in a Changing World* (CUP 2016) 172.

3 See also Meijers, who in his inaugural lecture in 1979 at the University of Amsterdam, argued that CIL was and would remain an important source of international law, and that its importance in fact has been growing rather than diminishing; H Meijers, 'How is International Law Made? – The Stages of Growth of International Law and the Use of its Customary Rules' (1978) 9 NYIL 3, 3–5; on the continuing importance and complexities of CIL see also L Lijnzaad and Council of Europe (eds), *The Judge and International Custom / Le juge et la coutume internationale* (Brill 2016); H Ruiz Fabri, *Sur quelques aspects de la théorie de la coutume en droit international contemporain* (Thèse soutenue en 1989 à Bordeaux 1).

4 ILC, 'Analytical Guide to the Work of the International Law Commission' (*ILC*, 2023) <https://legal.un.org/ilc/guide/gfra.shtml> last accessed 1 October 2023.

5 Both in the research on CIL and in other topics, such as immunities.

to the level, frequency and intensity that treaty interpretation has. It has to be noted that the main focus of this contribution is judicial interpretation of CIL. Although, undeniably, other actors may and have engaged in CIL interpretation, judicial interpretation was considered to be best suited to the aims of and questions to be addressed by this paper, namely whether CIL interpretation is from a theoretical standpoint possible, and whether it has been occurring in international and domestic judicial practice. Naturally, such an inquiry could extend to the actions and practice of other actors as well,[6] an interesting angle of inquiry undoubtedly but one that is sequential both temporally and logically to an examination of the interpretability of custom and which before being broached requires a foundation that this study aims to provide.[7]

Bearing these considerations in mind, Section 2 will inquire into the potential reasons why CIL interpretation has not received a similar attention and analysis as treaty interpretation. With respect to CIL one of the main assumptions, that this study challenges, is that identification, ie determining whether a rule exists or not, and content-determination, are one and the same thing.[8] Section 2 will closely scrutinize this and other main arguments usually put forth regarding the alleged non-interpretability of CIL, and examine whether such arguments are truly a bar to CIL interpretation or whether they collapse upon closer inspection. Section 2 will demonstrate that despite its unwritten nature, not only is CIL from a theoretical standpoint interpretable, but also that other non-written acts and instruments have been accepted as theoretically interpretable and have in practice been interpreted.

Following the analysis of Section 2 on whether there are any theoretical obstacles to the interpretability of CIL, and finding that there are none, in Sections 3 and 4 the study will turn to international and domestic case-law and identify repeated patterns, which judges follow when interpreting CIL. What will be shown is that in both international (Section 3) and domestic (Section 4) case-law there is a plethora of instances where CIL has clearly been the object of interpretation. The methods employed are methods that are, in general,

---

6 And such references when required by the corresponding analysis will be made, eg to the works of the ILC, of the *Institut de Droit International* and to statements of States.

7 For a recent foray into the interpretation of CIL rules by an international organisation, namely the EU, see P Merkouris, RA Wessel and IT de Vries-Zou (eds), *The European Union and the Interpretation of Customary International Law* (Asser Institute, CLEER Papers 2024/1) <https://www.asser.nl/media/796897/cleer_024-01_web-final.pdf> last accessed 1 October 2023.

8 On this point see also: R di Marco, 'Customary International Law: Identification versus Interpretation' in P Merkouris, J Kammerhoffer and N Arajärvi (eds), *The Theory, Practice and Interpretation of Customary International Law* (CUP 2022) 414; R di Marco, *L'interpretazione del diritto consuetudinario* (PhD Thesis, Università di Roma Tor Vergata / Université Paris Nanterre, November 2022) (on file with the author).

familiar and known to all users of international law from treaty interpretation. However, that is not to say that there is complete identity between the methods of interpretation of treaties and of customary rules. Despite some overlap there are at points certain differences in the content and manner of employment of such methods, that Sections 3 and 4 will highlight.

Any inquiry into interpretation always ends up with the question, whether there are limits to the interpretative discretion of judges. In order to answer this, one needs to examine whether one can talk of 'correct interpretation'. In Section 5 the study will delve into an examination of the premise of the 'correct interpretation' in public international law. Such a question is, of course, not source-specific, but is rather one that is tied to the characteristics of legal interpretation as a process. Nonetheless, or perhaps even because of this it is a necessary inquiry to be made, as a first step towards examining whether there are any limits to interpretation, in general, and then to the interpretation of CIL rules more concretely. Section 5 will demonstrate that we can talk about sets of correct and incorrect interpretations of international legal rules. This then raises the question of whether there are any rules or guidelines that demarcate at what point an interpretation of a legal rule moves from the set of correct interpretations to that of incorrect ones. Such limits will be identified in Section 6.

The remaining Sections will then elaborate on whether the limits discussed in Section 6, can be transposed to the interpretation of CIL rules. Three are the main limits that will be examined: *jus cogens* norms (Section 7), revision (Section 8) and finally the rules of interpretation themselves, or simply put misinterpretation (Section 9).

Having examined all these issues the study will conclude in Section 10 as to whether CIL can be interpreted and what are the methods and limits of such an interpretative exercise. In an Annex, the 2023 TRICI-Law Draft Guiding Principles on the Interpretation of Rules of Customary International Law are reproduced.

2 Interpretation of Customary International Law: Barred Due to Its Nature, or a Valid Method of Content-Determination?

Everyone involved with international law is familiar with the classical two-element approach to CIL, famously stated in the *North Sea Continental Shelf* cases.[9] The vast majority of the literature has been devoted to restating, refining

9 *North Sea Continental Shelf (Germany/Denmark and the Netherlands)* (Judgment) [1969] ICJ Rep 3 [77].

or criticising the various pitfalls of the objective and subjective/psychological elements.[10] However, the present contribution does not aim to engage with the wider *problématique* of the two elements, but rather whether the content-determination of CIL can only be understood and accomplished only through those two elements, or also through a process that we are more familiar with as interpretation.

During 2013–2018 the ILC revisited this source of international law. Originally, the title of the topic was 'Formation and Evidence of Customary International Law',[11] but following debate within the ILC and informal consultations it was changed to 'Identification of Customary International Law'.[12] This was done due to practical considerations as the term 'evidence' posed difficulties in being translated into the other official United Nations (UN) languages, but also in order to emphasise that the 'principal objective of the topic was to offer guidance to those called upon to identify the existence of a rule of customary international law', with the focus being on the 'two-element approach' and the 'formative elements' of CIL.[13] What this had as a natural consequence is that the ILC's main focus, as can also be seen by the Draft Conclusions,[14] was on the two elements and how these are to be identified and evaluated. In this the ILC seems to have also somewhat taken the approach that 'the questions of whether a rule of customary law exists, and how customary law is made, tend

10 Indicatively: M Akehurst, 'Custom as a Source of International Law' (1977) 47 BYIL 1; M Bos, 'The Identification of Custom in International Law' (1982) 25 GYIL 9; P Haggenmacher, 'La doctrine des deux éléments du droit coutumier dans la pratique de la Cour internationale' (1986) 90 RGDIP 5; O Elias and CL Lim, *The Paradox of Consensualism in International Law* (Kluwer Law International 1998); M Byers, *Custom, Power and the Power of Rules: International Rules and Customary International Law* (CUP 1999)130–3; I Brownlie, 'Some Problems in the Evaluation of the Practice of States as an Element of Custom' in G Arangio-Ruiz (ed), *Studi di diritto internazionale in onore di Gaetano Arangio-Ruiz, Vol I* (Editoriale Scientifica 2004) 313; Ph Pazartzis, 'Le rôle de la pratique dans le droit coutumier' in RH Vinaixa (ed), *L' influence des sources sur l' unité et la fragmentation du droit international* (Bruylant 2006) 81; JL Goldsmith and EA Posner, *Limits of International Law* (OUP 2007) 3–78; S Droubi and J d'Aspremont (eds), *International Organisations, Non-state Actors, and the Formation of Customary International Law* (MUP 2020); M Hakimi, 'Making Sense of Customary International Law' (2020) 118/8 MichLRev 1487.

11 ILC, 'First Report on Formation and Evidence of Customary International Law, by Sir Michael Wood, Special Rapporteur' (17 May 2013) UN Doc A/CN.4/663.

12 ILC, 'Second Report on Identification of Customary International Law, by Michael Wood, Special Rapporteur' (22 May 2014) UN Doc A/CN.4/672.

13 Ibid [2].

14 ILC, 'Draft Conclusions on Identification of Customary International Law, with Commentaries' (30 April–10 August 2018) UN Doc A/73/10, reproduced in [2018/II – Part Two] YBILC 122.

in practice to coalesce'.[15] However, there are two issues with this. First, 'tend' does not mean that this is always the case, as will become clear in the Sections below. Second, and more importantly, this seems to somewhat conflate the emergence/formation of CIL with its content-determination. It is true that some level of content-determination will occur at the level of identification of the 'formative elements', but that is not, as will be demonstrated below, the only venue of content-determination of CIL. To say that identifying State practice and *opinio juris* is the be all end all of CIL would be a gross oversimplification both from a methodological and a practice-focused evaluation.

In fact, this was the exact point raised by the Netherlands, when governments were asked to comment on the Draft Conclusions of the ILC.

> The draft conclusions and the related commentary frequently refer to the identification or determination of the 'existence and content' of customary international law. It does not become clear whether the process for identifying the existences of a rule is the same as the process for determining the content of that rule. In our view, this is not necessarily the case. For example, in the identification of the content of a particular rule, any underlying principles of international law may need to be taken into account in accordance with draft conclusion 3(1), whereas this may not be the case when identifying the existence of the rule. We suggest it would be helpful to make this explicit in the commentary.[16]

In this the Netherlands followed very closely the advice of its Advisory Committee on Issues of Public International Law (CAVV), some additional comments of which also help further clarify this point. According to CAVV, '[i]t may be wondered, for example, *whether the unity and coherence of the system of international law* to which the ILC refers … does not require *that rules of customary international law be interpreted in their mutual context*. Reference could be made, for example, to the considerations of the International Court of Justice (ICJ) in the *Asylum Case*, in which it held that the possibility of granting diplomatic asylum would derogate from the sovereignty and territorial jurisdiction

15 ILC 'Second Report' (n 12) [2] note 6; citing in support R Jennings, 'What is International Law and how do we Tell it When we See it?' (1981) 37 Annuaire Suisse de Droit International 59, 59–60 and K Wolfke, *Custom in Present International Law* (2nd edn, Brill/Martinus Nijhoff 1993) 116.

16 Netherlands, 'ILC Draft Conclusions on the Identification of Customary International Law – Comments and Observations by the Kingdom of the Netherlands' (UN, 2018) <https://legal.un.org/ilc/sessions/70/pdfs/english/icil_netherlands.pdf> [5] last accessed 1 October 2023.

of a State … and in the *Jurisdictional Immunities of the State Case*, in which it construed the immunity rules in conjunction with the underlying rule of territorial jurisdiction … In short, the Committee believes it *would be desirable to make this distinction explicit or in any event to bear it in mind. There are various processes which are or could be applicable to determining the existence of a rule of customary international law on the one hand and its content on the other*'.[17]

Furthermore, the ILC too in a different and more recent research topic, that of immunities, made this equally abundantly clear. On a topic such as immunities that is in its very core a CIL issue, the reports by *Special Rapporteur* Concepción Escobar Hernández are full of references to the inevitability and utility of CIL interpretation for the purpose of clarifying the content of the CIL rules on immunities.[18]

This debate is reflective of a wider discussion surrounding CIL and its interpretation. Bos famously wrote that in the case of CIL, there is no need to engage with interpretation since 'content merges with existence'[19] and, thus, the mere application of the two-element approach in and of itself provides all the content-determination required for a CIL rule to be applicable in any given situation.[20] This is by no means an undisputed claim.[21] The ILC's work

17 Advisory Committee on Issues of Public International Law (CAVV), 'Advisory Report on the Identification of Customary International Law' (*CAVV*, 2017) <https://www.advisorycommitteeinternationallaw.nl/binaries/cavv-en/documenten/advisory-reports/2017/11/01/the-identification-of-customary-international-law/The_identification_of_customary_international_law_CAVV-Advisory-report-29_201711.PDF> Sct 2.2 last accessed 1 October 2023 (emphasis added).

18 ILC, 'Fifth Report on Immunity of State Officials from Foreign Criminal Jurisdiction, by Concepción Escobar Hernández, Special Rapporteur' (14 June 2016) UN Doc A/CN.4/701 [150]. The specific methods of interpretation and limits that the report alludes to will be analysed in more detail below in the corresponding Sections.

19 M Bos, *A Methodology of International Law* (Elsevier Science Publisher BV 1984) 109.

20 Similarly, disputing the interpretability of CIL, see T Treves, 'Customary International Law' [2006] MPEPIL 1393 [2]; VD Degan, *L'interprétation des accords en droit international* (Nijhoff 1963) 162; M Lando, 'Identification as the Process to Determine the Content of Customary International Law' (2022) 42/4 OJLS 1040–66 (although in more recent writings this last author seems to have moved away from the outright rejection of CIL interpretation; see M Lando, 'Might It Just Work? How To Interpret Customary International Law (Maybe)' (*CIL Dialogues*, 6 March 2023) <https://cil.nus.edu.sg/blogs/might-it-just-work-how-to-interpret-customary-international-law-maybe/> last accessed 31 October 2023).

21 P Merkouris, *Article 31(3)(c) and the Principle of Systemic Integration: Normative Shadows in Plato's Cave* (Brill/Nijhoff 2015) ch 4; Ph Allot, 'Interpretation – an Exact Art' in A Bianchi, D Peat and M Windsor (eds), *Interpretation in International Law* (OUP 2015) 373, 385–6; D Alland, 'L' interprétation du droit international public' (2013) 362 RdC 1, 82–8; A Orakhelashvili, *The Interpretation of Acts and Rules in Public International Law* (OUP 2008) ch 15; R Kolb, *Interprétation et création du droit international: esquisses d' une herméneutique*

on immunities, and the comments and practice of States (as shall be shown in the following Sections, in addition to the ones already mentioned) take the position that interpretation has been, continues to and will always be an integral part of the life-cycle of CIL rules, as of any legal rule for that matter. Sur, in fact, has very eloquently suggested that interpretation of CIL is perhaps even more noteworthy than treaty interpretation. Whereas, in his view, treaty interpretation is entropic, '[t]he interpretation of custom is creative or negentropic [ie reduces entropy], because it constantly nourishes and updates it [ie CIL], softening the distinction between formation and application'.[22]

There is no point in debating assertive or axiomatic statements[23] regarding the interpretability or not of CIL. The former not being methodologically relevant,[24] while the latter are by definition non-falsifiable, ie they cannot be demonstrated to be wrong. If they are falsifiable and falsified, as this study will strive to do in the course of our analysis with respect to the arguments on non-interpretability of CIL, they are not true axioms, but rather pseudo-axioms. For this reason, this study will focus its attention to the more substantiated arguments that have been proposed and which allegedly demonstrate why interpretation is irrelevant in the case of CIL.

The most often and obvious contestation regarding CIL's interpretability is that its rules are non-written. As Treves notes 'the irrelevance of linguistic expression *excludes interpretation as a necessary operation* in order to apply

juridique moderne pour le droit international public (Bruylant 2006) 219 et seq; A Bleckmann, 'Zur Feststellung und Auslegung von Völkergewohnheitsrecht' (1977) 37 ZaöRV 504; G Barile, 'La rilevazione e l'integrazione del diritto internazionale non scritto e la libertà di apprezzamento del giudice' (1953) 5 Comunicazioni e studi 141; LM Bentivoglio, 'Per una interpretazione funzionale del diritto internazionale' [1965] Annuario di diritto internazionale 32, 35. For an interpretation of customary law from a domestic perspective see also P Staubach, 'The Interpretation of Unwritten International Law by Domestic Judges' in HP Aust and G Nolte (eds), *The Interpretation of International Law by Domestic Courts: Unity, Diversity, Convergence* (OUP 2016) 113, 120.

22 S Sur, 'La créativité du droit international' (2013) 363 RdC 9, 295 (author's translation).

23 Assertion, in the case of CIL, refers to when the existence and/or content of a customary rule is stated without offering though any analysis on why this is so; see S Talmon, 'Determining Customary International Law: The ICJ's Methodology between Induction, Deduction and Assertion' (2005) 26(2) EJIL 417; an axiomatic statement is a statement that reflects an axiom, ie a universally accepted and general truth, and cannot be proven or disproven (falsified).

24 On the former being not methodologically relevant, see O Sender and M Wood, 'The International Court of Justice and Customary International Law: A Reply to Stefan Talmon' (*EJILTalk!*, 30 November 2015) <https://www.ejiltalk.org/the-international-court-of-justice-and-customary-international-law-a-reply-to-stefan-talmon/> last accessed 1 October 2023.

[customary rules]'.[25] To this one could easily respond with Alland's insightful remark, who notes that 'it is difficult to think of a custom independently of any linguistic expression, of any "lexical garment", to use [Müller's] wonderful expression. In fact, even if we do not put the customary rule in a codification convention, it must be formulated and, from this formulation, it may appear that we are interpreting linguistic signs expressing a customary rule'.[26] This seems to be also a pattern that comes up time and time again in international and domestic jurisprudence (as shown in Sections 3 and 4).

However, even if one leaves considerations of CIL having a 'lexical garment' aside, the argument 'on linguistic irrelevance' still fails to stand up to scrutiny for both reasons of logic and existing international practice. Let us start from logic. Here, two are the main issues. First, it seems to be predicated on an understanding of the interpretative process as one that is entirely dominated by the text. Indeed, text is an important element in the interpretative process. However, as a simple perusal of Articles 31–3 of the Vienna Convention on the Law of Treaties (VCLT) clearly demonstrates, text is but one of the elements that the interpreter can take into account, with a wide gamut of non-textual elements featuring prominently. Furthermore, similarly to the ILC, international courts and tribunals, and States have also on multiple occasions very explicitly stated that the approach taken in interpretation of international rules is the 'crucible approach',[27] ie that all the elements are taken into together with no pre-existing hierarchy, and this process leads to the correct interpretation.[28]

A second logical argument that militates in favour of the non-written nature of a rule being irrelevant for the purposes of interpretation is of an *ad absurdum* type. It is well known that rules in international law may exist at the same time both as a CIL rule and as a conventional rule.[29] Let us hypothesise that these two rules are identical. If, however, interpretation were to be accepted only for written rules, then only the conventional rule would be open

---

25 Treves (n 20) [2] (emphasis added).

26 Alland (n 21) 83 referring to F Müller, *Discours de la méthode juridique* (O Jouanjan tr, Presses Universitaires de France 1996) 171 and Kolb (n 21) 221. However, see also Kammerhofer's analysis that CIL 'is not couched in words – *sine letteris*'; J Kammerhofer, *International Investment Law and Legal Theory* (CUP 2021) 77.

27 ILC, 'Draft Articles on the Law of Treaties with Commentaries' (4 May–19 July 1966) UN Doc A/CN.4/191, reproduced in [1966/II] YBILC 187, 220 [8].

28 On the issue of 'correct interpretation' see below Sections 5 and 6, and in more detail: P Merkouris, 'The Correct Interpretation Premise in International Adjudication' in P Westerman, K Gorobets and A Hadjigeorgiou (eds), *Conceptual (De)Constructions of International Law* (Edward Elgar 2022) 215–33.

29 *Military and Paramilitary Activities in and against Nicaragua* (*Nicaragua v* USA) (Merits) [1986] ICJ Rep 14 [175–8].

to interpretation. In that rule's case the interpreter would be able to utilise the entire arsenal of interpretative tools in order to determine the content of the rule, eg object and purpose, intent, other relevant rules and any of the other elements enshrined in Articles 31–3 VCLT. The CIL rule, on the other hand, would benefit from none or almost none of the above. In each and every case, it would have to be determined entirely on the basis of an evaluation of relevant State practice and *opinio juris*. This would lead to a situation, where despite the rules having the same starting point and content, the conventional rule would have the potential of being further refined as to its content through the process of interpretation, whereas the CIL rule would not. Similarly, whereas the conventional rule through a teleological or evolutive interpretation could adapt to new situations, the CIL rule would not unless very explicit and relevant State practice existed but that is almost never the situation. This means that the classical law ascertainment scheme, focusing entirely on State practice and *opinio juris*, does not allow for adaptation to new and/or changes circumstances or at least not with the veracity and vivacity that evolutive interpretation allows treaty rules to adapt.

This seems to be an illogical result that ends treating legal rules of the same normative value differently for no apparent reason. Germany's 2021 position paper 'On the Application of International Law in Cyberspace' is based precisely on this point.[30] The need to allow CIL through interpretation to adapt to new circumstances and situations. Despite the fact that there is not sufficient practice as to the application of international humanitarian law (IHL) principles in the cyberspace, Germany made an official statement to the effect that this was not problematic. In fact, Germany was 'convinced that uncertainties as to how international law [and CIL in particular, since the report was devoted to CIL] might be applied in the cyber *context can and must be addressed by having recourse to the established methods of interpretation of international law*'.[31] This is far from the only example. International and domestic judicial practice offer up a veritable *smörgåsbord*[32] of instances where interpretation was far from immaterial in the case of CIL rules, as will be shown in Sections 3–4 and 7–9.

A final point that needs to be raised in this context is that interpretation of non-written elements is not so exotic as the 'linguistic irrelevance' argument

30 Germany, 'On the Application of International Law in Cyberspace – Position Paper' (*Auswärtiges Amt*, March 2021) <https://www.auswaertiges-amt.de/blob/2446304/32e7b2498e10b74fb17204c54665bdf0/on-the-application-of-international-law-in-cyberspace-data.pdf> 16, last accessed 1 October 2023.

31 Ibid (emphasis added).

32 *Smörgåsbord*, stemming from Swedish, and which literally refers to a buffet-style meal with multiple choices, is used here to refer to a plethora of instances.

would seem to suggest. Two are the most notable examples: non-written agreements and unilateral acts of States creating international obligations. Although non-written/oral agreements were more common in the pre-Westphalian era, and are nowadays in considerable decline,[33] they still happen from time to time, as in the case of the Ihlen Declaration[34] and the telephone agreement of 1992 between the prime ministers of Denmark and Finland regarding the Great Belt Bridge.[35] The binding character of oral treaties, or verbal treaties or verbal/oral agreements as they are sometimes called,[36] has been well recognised in international jurisprudence, as was the case in *Mavrommatis Jerusalem Concessions*.[37] Their binding character was also uncontroversial during the ILC discussions on the law of treaties.[38] Although Article 2(1)(a) VCLT makes no specific reference to such treaties, focusing rather on treaties in written form,[39]

33 K Schmalenbach, 'Article 3' in O Dörr and K Schmalenbach (eds), *Vienna Convention on the Law of Treaties: A Commentary* (Springer 2018) 55, 57 [5].

34 M Fitzmaurice and P Merkouris, *Treaties in Motion: The Evolution of Treaties from Formation to Termination* (CUP 2020) 48–51. It still unclear whether this was indeed an oral agreement or a set of unilateral obligations creating mutually binding international obligations; see ILC, 'Summary Record of the 668th Meeting' (26 June 1962) UN Doc A/CN.4/SR.668 [156]; K Widdows, 'On the Form and Distinctive Nature of International Agreements' (1981) 7(1) Australian YBIL 114, 119.

35 M Koskenniemi, 'Introductory Note: International Court of Justice: Order Discontinuing the Proceedings in *Case Concerning Passage Through the Great Belt (Finland v Denmark)*' (1993) 32 ILM 101, 103 [9]; further examples can be found in Y le Bouthillier and J-F Bonin, 'Article 3 – Convention of 1969' in O Corten and P Klein (eds), *The Vienna Convention on the Law of Treaties: A Commentary* (OUP 2011) 66, 70–1 [11] and note 27; X Qin, 'Oral International Agreement and China's Relevant Practice' (2005) 4/2 Chinese Journal of International Law 465, 472–6.

36 The use of the term agreement is sometimes preferred to avoid the connection with the term treaty as specified in the VCLT, which has as a required element the written form as per Art 2(1)(a) VCLT.

37 *The Mavrommatis Jerusalem Concessions (Greece v the United Kingdom)* [1925] PCIJ Rep Ser A No 5, 37.

38 ILC 'Draft Articles on the Law of Treaties with Commentaries' (n 27) 190, Commentary to Draft Article 3, [3]; ILC, 'First Report on the Law of Treaties by Sir Humphrey Waldock, Special Rapporteur' (26 March 1962) UN Doc A/CN.4/144 and Add.1 reproduced in [1962/II] YBILC 27, 35 [2].

39 Although it has taken a rather broad approach as to the 'written form' requirement. For instance, even oral agreements that are evidenced in writing, as in the case of an oral agreement that is documented by a third party, so authorized by the parties to the agreement are considered to satisfy the 'written form' requirement; P Gautier, 'Article 2 – Convention of 1969' in O Corten and P Klein (eds), *The Vienna Convention on the Law of Treaties: A Commentary* (OUP 2011) 33, 39 [16]. However, if no such authorized transcription exists (the examples usually given are those of (video)-taped understandings or oral answers to written proposals) these remain oral agreements; ILC, 'Report on the Law of Treaties

a choice mandated for reasons of clarity and simplicity,[40] Article 3 VCLT clearly stipulates that although the VCLT does not apply to international agreements not in written form, this does not affect the binding effect of such agreements or the application to them of CIL rules on the law of treaties.[41] Since, then, the CIL rules on the law of treaties are applicable to oral treaties as long as they are not affected by their non-written nature, and since interpretation is far from entirely based on textuality,[42] the customary rules on treaty interpretation would be equally applicable *mutatis mutandis*.[43]

The same conclusion was arrived at by the ILC with respect to unilateral acts of States creating international obligations. This was a topic that the ILC worked on for a decade (1996–2006). Following the ICJ's judgment in *Nuclear Tests*,[44] the ILC adopted Guiding Principle 5 which clarified that the form of such acts, ie whether oral in writing, was immaterial for the purposes of the application of the Guiding Principles.[45] This is notable as Guiding Principle 7 was devoted to the interpretation of such, again making no distinction whatsoever as to whether the declaration is oral or in writing.[46] Consequently, interpretation of non-written instruments and acts, other than CIL rules, is nothing either unusual or unheard of in international law.[47]

---

by Mr GG Fitzmaurice' (14 March 1956) UN Doc A/CN.4/101 reproduced in [1956/II] YBILC 104, 117 note 4.

40 ILC, 'Draft Articles on the Law of Treaties' (24 April–29 June 1962) UN Doc A/5209 reproduced in [1962/II] YBILC 161, 163 [10]; K Schmalenbach, 'Article 2' in O Dörr and K Schmalenbach (eds), *Vienna Convention on the Law of Treaties: A Commentary* (2nd edn, Springer 2018) 29, 36 [19]; M Villiger, *Commentary on the 1969 Vienna Convention on the Law of Treaties* (Brill/Nijhoff 2008) 80 [15]; M Fitzmaurice, 'The Identification and Character of Treaties and Treaty Obligations Between States in International Law' (2002) 73 BYIL 141, 149; le Bouthillier and Bonin (n 35) 71.

41 Art 3 VCLT; see also ILC, "Draft Articles on the Law of Treaties with Commentaries' (n 27) 189 [7].

42 See Arts 31–3 VCLT.

43 Schmalenbach (n 33) 58 [7]; M Herdegen, 'Interpretation in International Law' [2013] MPEPIL 723 [2].

44 *Nuclear Tests* (*Australia v France*) (Judgment) [1974] ICJ Rep 253 [45] (emphasis added).

45 ILC, 'Guiding Principles Applicable to Unilateral Declarations of States Capable of Creating Legal Obligations with Commentaries Thereto' (1 May–9 June and 3 July–11 August 2006) UN Doc A/61/10 reproduced in [2006/II – Part Two] YBILC 160, Guiding Principle 5.

46 Ibid 173 et seq; Guiding Principle 7.

47 Other notable examples from the work of the ILC where interpretation of non-written rules is either explicitly accepted or a necessary premise, are: ILC, 'Draft Conclusions on Identification and Legal Consequences of Peremptory Norms of General International Law (Jus Cogens), with Commentaries' (2022) UN Doc A/77/10, Draft Conclusion 20 and accompanying Commentary (analysed in more detail below in Section 7); ILC, 'Fifth Report' (n 18) (analysed in this Section and Section 7); and ILC, 'Draft Conclusions on CIL Identification' (n 14) Draft Conclusion 3 (analysed in this Section).

So, let us then examine another line of argumentation against the interpretability of CIL. One that has already been mentioned above is that 'content merges with existence'.[48] The crux of this argument is that the application of the two-element approach will in every imaginable situation satisfy the level of content-determination necessary for the CIL rule to be applied. This seems, however, to overestimate the degree of specificity that State practice may offer. Given that for the emergence of a CIL rule what is required is widespread, representative, consistent, virtually uniform State practice accompanied by *opinio juris*,[49] it seems highly unlikely, especially for newly emergent situations, that these elements would meet the threshold required. Once again, Germany's position paper on the applicability of CIL on IHL in cyberspace raises precisely this point, ie that CIL needs to adapt to new situations, and this can only be done through the process of interpretation.[50] As Sur noted in his General Course in the Hague Academy of International the importance of CIL interpretation is paramount because '[i]nterpretation of customary rules allows the formulation of a statement that specifies their content and meaning'.[51]

Given the fact that CIL is often criticised as being vague[52] it seems not only counter-intuitive but blatantly illogical to require from rules emerging from this source a level of specificity and precision, that no one expects even from written instruments. As written laws are seen as 'living trees' that are open to evolution, mainly though evolutive interpretation, in order to adapt to new circumstances so the same must be true, if not even more so, in the case of CIL rules. This also seems to be the rationale behind the ICJ's pronouncement in *Gulf of Maine* that '[a] body of detailed rules is not to be looked for in customary international law' and that rather in order to address all potentially arising situation (on delimitation in that case) the Court should through interpretation 'seek a better formulation of the fundamental norm'.[53]

---

48 Bos (n 19) 109.

49 ILC, 'Draft Conclusions on CIL Identification' (n 14) Draft Conclusion 8 and accompanying commentary; see also indicatively: *North Sea Continental Shelf* (n 9) [74]; *Asylum Case (Colombia/Peru)* [1950] ICJ Rep 266, 277.

50 Germany (n 30).

51 Sur 'La créativité' (n 22).

52 ILA, 'Final Report of the Committee – Statement of Principles Applicable to the Formation of General Customary International Law' (2000) 69 ILARC 712, 713.

53 *Delimitation of the Maritime Boundary in the Gulf of Maine Area (Canada v USA)* (Merits) [184] ICJ Rep 246 [111] (emphasis added).

Another argument tied to the 'content merges with existence' line of reasoning is that there is no exact law-creating moment for CIL.[54] Because of this, so the argument goes, CIL rules need always be determined by reference to State practice and *opinio juris*. However, two objections need to be raised with respect to this argument. First, the lack of an 'exact' law-creating moment is not the same as that there is no law-creating moment (or at least time-period). Taking a cue from philosophy, this seems to be very similar to the *sorites* paradox. Just because one cannot pinpoint exactly when the collection/set of grains of sand[55] turns into a *sorites* that does not mean that the *sorites* does not exist.[56]

Although, there will be a grey area where it will be difficult to determine whether a *sorites*, or in our case a CIL rule has emerged or not, on both sides of this grey area, there will be others where the CIL clearly has not emerged, and where it has. One does not need to look too far, and this is the second objection. Take, for instance, the numerous cases where the international courts and tribunals have not even bothered establishing the CIL nature of certain legal rules, by virtue of considering them as well-established.[57] One may not be certain when exactly they emerged, and for the most part, unless there are *ratione temporis* considerations in play, that will be immaterial for the judges, but as long as the CIL rule exists now (or during the period relevant for the dispute) that suffices.

A potential way to try and salvage the 'lack of exact law-creating moment' argument may be that even when one knows that a CIL rule is established, the interpreter will always look again at State practice and *opinio juris* to see if the rule has developed or been modified. However, this does not seem to be supported by practice, since often courts and tribunals do not engage in such a process but dive directly into interpretative considerations, looking eg at the teleology, rationale or the normative background of the CIL rule, as shown in

---

54 J d' Aspremont, 'Custom-making Moment in Customary International Law' in P Merkouris, J Kammerhofer and N Arajärvi, *The Theory, Practice and Interpretation of Customary International Law* (CUP 2022) 29.

55 Or seeds depending on the example.

56 In more detail on the *sorites* paradox see D Hyde and D Raffman, 'Sorites Paradox' (*Stanford Encyclopedia of Philosophy*, 26 March 2018) <https://plato.stanford.edu/entries/sorites-paradox/> last accessed 1 October 2023; R Sorensen, *A Brief History of the Paradox: Philosophy and the Labyrinths of the Mind* (OUP 2003), 52–4, 96–8 and 122.

57 As it is considered a given due to numerous cases that have already established it and the acceptance and even in some cases invocation by the States themselves in international proceedings. Take, for instance, rules of interpretation, or certain state responsibility rules. See, eg, *Maritime Delimitation in the Indian Ocean* (*Somalia v Kenya*) (Preliminary Objections) [2017] ICJ Rep 3 [63]; *Jadhav* (*India v Pakistan*) (Judgment) [2019] ICJ Rep 418 [71]. For such and other examples see Sections 3–4 below.

Sections 3–4. Furthermore, even when such an action is taken by the judges/interpreters this is not an obstacle to CIL interpretation. If the judge examines State practice to determine whether anything new has been added to the content of the rule, s/he may conclude that this is not the case, but then questions will arise as to whether the interpretation of the CIL rule allows for that rule to be applicable in the case in question.[58] As to whether the rule has been modified/revised again this is nothing unfamiliar. Even in treaties this is a process that naturally occurs, and it is more about considerations of the limits of interpretation (see Section 6), but again it is not a bar to interpretation.

In sum, the 'content merges with existence' line of thought fails on multiple fronts. First, it fails to account for how CIL can be applicable to newly emergent situations. Not allowing CIL interpretation, then this would mean that CIL becomes static and ossified, whereas interpretation breathes life into it and introduces a 'negentropic process'.[59] Second, it cannot explain the content-determination of well-established CIL rules, where courts and tribunals do not refer to State practice or *opinio juris* but rather apply classical interpretative tools. Third, it conflates law-ascertainment with content-determination. Although there may be some overlap, and necessarily any determination regarding the existence or not of a CIL rule will have some interpretative aspects, these two processes should not be confused, because not only are they not identical but they also have different objectives, and are governed by different rules.[60]

58 See, for instance, Germany (n 30); see also examples in Sections 3–4 and 7–9.

59 Entropy is often used to refer to the degree of disorder or randomness of a complex system, and is viewed as a quantity that only increases with time. Negentropy, thus, should be seen as entropy in the opposite direction, ie from a state of disorder and chaotic randomness gradually over time moving to a state of order 9 of varying degrees). Thus, in Sur's view, CIL interpretation has this negentropic quality.

60 Hollis, when discussing such interpretative elements existing in the identification of a rule, adopts the term 'existential interpretation' which he defines as the process through which one determines whether a rule exists or not. According to Hollis, such an 'existential interpretation' is binary in nature. Either the rule exists or not. DB Hollis, 'The Existential Function of Interpretation in International Law' in A Bianchi, D Peat and M Windsor (eds), *Interpretation in International Law* (OUP 2015) 78, 79–87. This should be clearly distinguished from interpretation proper, which is not binary but rather a spectrum. For this reason, and in order to avoid confusion between the two processes (a point that is also repeated below in the discussion of 'interpretation of State practice') it makes more sense to not use the term 'interpretation' at the level of identification of rule and a CIL rule in our case. The need to avoid confusion is also evident in Guiding Principle 7 of the 'Guiding Principles applicable to unilateral declarations of States capable of creating legal obligations' and Draft Conclusion 3 of the ILC Draft Conclusions on CIL, discussed in more detail below in this Section (see nn 60–4 and corresponding main text).

Draft Conclusion 3 of the ILC Draft Conclusions on CIL is a prime example of this. Draft Conclusion 3 provides that '[i]n assessing evidence for the purpose of ascertaining whether there is a general practice and whether that practice is accepted as law (*opinio juris*), regard *must be had to the overall context, the nature of the rule* and the particular circumstances in which the evidence in question is to be found'.[61] Even if one accepts that the 'assessment of State practice' includes the wider normative environment (which in this author's view is in reality a 'systemic integration' type of interpretation),[62] that still does not account for the wide gamut of other interpretative tools used, such a *telos*, rationale,[63] *effet utile* etc (for more, see Sections 3–4). This is exactly why the Netherlands made the aforementioned comment regarding the need to clarify the content-determinative process as distinct from mere identification. Furthermore, the fact that rules should not be interpreted in a vacuum, is also something that happens in the case of treaties. In fact, it happens in all stages of the treaty's 'life-cycle', as can be seen, for instance, with respect to grounds of nullity and termination as well as to the doctrine of intertemporal law, the latter being relevant not only for determining the continued manifestation of a right or obligation, but also for its interpretation.[64] Consequently, even if taking into account the 'normative environment' may be relevant for identifying the existence of a rule, this does not bar it being relevant in other stages of the 'life-cycle' of CIL. As will be shown below, it can and has a significant role to play in the interpretative stage as well. Consideration and assessment of State practice and *opinio juris* can only take one so far down the content-determinative path. In order to ensure the effectiveness and relevance of CIL rules, as of any legal rule, interpretation is inevitable.[65]

---

61 ILC 'Draft Conclusions on CIL Identification' (n 14) Draft Conclusion 3 (emphasis added).

62 See in detail, below Section 3; see also TRICI-Law, 'Draft Guiding Principles on the Interpretation of Customary International Law' (*TRICI-Law*, 2023) Guiding Principles 6 and 9 and accompanying Commentaries, <https://tricilawofficial.wordpress.com/draftprinciples/> last accessed 1 October 2023 (hereinafter TRICI-Law Guiding Principles on CIL Interpretation).

63 See in detail, below Sections 3–4. See also TRICI-Law Guiding Principles on CIL Interpretation (n 62), Guiding Principle 5 and accompanying Commentary.

64 Fitzmaurice and Merkouris (n 34), chs 4–6.

65 Guiding Principle 7 of the 'Guiding Principles applicable to unilateral declarations of States capable of creating legal obligations' is also another interesting example in this context. Guiding Principle 7 states: 'A unilateral declaration entails obligations for the formulating State only if it is stated in clear and specific terms. *In the case of doubt as to the scope of the obligations resulting from such a declaration, such obligations must be interpreted in a restrictive manner. In interpreting the content of such obligations, weight shall be given first and foremost to the text of the declaration, together with the context and the circumstances in which it was formulated*' (emphasis added); ILC, 'Guiding Principles Applicable

That is not to say that this is a strictly linear process, ie first emergence of a rule, then interpretation, and then modification/revision or even termination. Drawing inspiration from quantum mechanics, the content of a legal rule at any given moment can be viewed as a field of superimposed potentialities.[66] As a particle in quantum mechanics exists in a state of superposition of several *eigenstates* until it is measured, so in our case, the legal rule[67] or at least the disputed part of its content also exists in a similar state of superposition. Hart, describing this somewhat differently and perhaps a bit more statically, referred to a rule's 'penumbra of uncertainty'.[68] Continuing the quantum analogy, at the moment of measurement, the wavefunction collapses into a single *eigenstate* and is thus 'pinned down' or concretized. In a similar fashion, interpretation performs much the same function. Each incident of judicial interpretation can be viewed as an instance where the quantum 'penumbra of uncertainty', transforms from a field of superimposed potentialities into a single reality by virtue of the act of interpretation (the 'observer' or 'act of measurement' to be more precise, if one wants to follow through with the double-slit experiment analogy).[69]

---

to Unilateral Declarations' (n 45), Guiding Principle 7. The second sentence referring to the 'scope of obligations' and adopting a restrictive interpretation, seems to conflict with the third sentence and the overall discussions within the ILC, where the VCLT rules on treaty interpretation were considered to apply *mutatis mutandis*, when determining the 'content' of such obligations. This confusion between 'scope' and 'content' can be resolved, if one considers the second sentence as referring to the identification of whether an obligation exists or not, whereas the third sentence refers to interpretation proper of the rule. It is again for these reasons of avoid confusion, that it is better to use a term other than 'interpretation' to describe the former process.

66 On superposition, the famous 'double-slit experiment' and the Copenhagen interpretation see J Faye, 'Copenhagen Interpretation of Quantum Mechanics' (*Stanford Encyclopedia of Philosophy*, 6 December 2019) <https://plato.stanford.edu/entries/qm-copenhagen/> last accessed 1 October 2023.

67 And for the purposes of the present study the CIL rule.

68 HLA Hart, *The Concept of Law* (3rd edn, OUP 2012) 124–36.

69 As noted elsewhere, this 'analogy seems to hold up irrespective of whether one adheres to the, for [the] purposes [of this study] serendipitously named, Copenhagen *interpretation* or alternative theories, such as the "pilot wave" theory'; P Merkouris and N Mileva, 'Introduction to the Series: Customary Law Interpretation as a Tool' (2022) 11/1 ESIL Reflections 1, 6 (*ESIL Reflections*, 1 August 2022) <https://esil-sedi.eu/wp-content/uploads/2022/08/ESIL-Reflection-Merkouris-Mileva.pdf> last accessed 1 October 2023. On 'pilot wave theory' as an alternative to the Copenhagen interpretation, see Sh Goldstein, 'Bohmian Mechanics' (*Stanford Encyclopedia of Philosophy*, 14 June 2021) <https://plato.stanford.edu/entries/qm-bohm/> last accessed 1 October 2023.

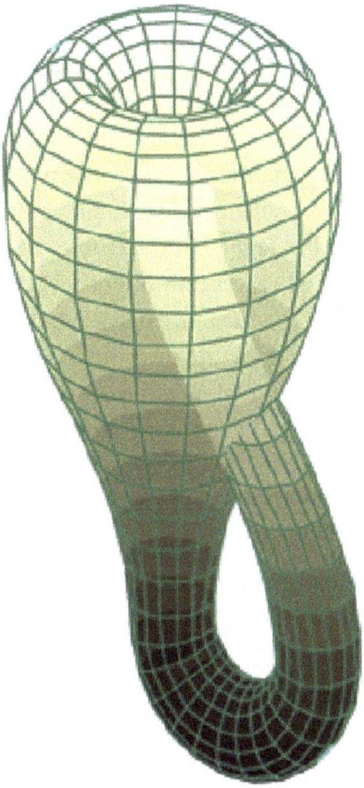

FIGURE 1
CIL as a Klein bottle
SOURCE: HTTPS://EN.WIKIPEDIA.ORG/WIKI/KLEIN_BOTTLE#/MEDIA/FILE:KLEIN_BOTTLE.SVG

Furthermore, each instance of CIL interpretation by domestic courts, in and of itself can also qualify as State practice.[70] This then may feed back into content-determination exercises, which can in turn lead to further clarifications, further restatements of the same interpretation, and if achieving critical mass eventually removal of that particular interpretation from the 'penumbra of uncertainty' to the 'core of settled application of the rule' to use Hart's famous statement. In this sense, although the various stages of the life-cycle of CIL are critically different from one another, they are not linear, but may loop back onto themselves. In this sense the CIL process resembles a Klein bottle (Figure 1).

Consequently, none of the main arguments that have been proposed as obstacles to the interpretability of CIL, seem to be truly prohibitive of such an endeavour. Before I proceed to an examination of relevant international and

70 Or in the case of international judicial pronouncements a supplementary means for the determination of a CIL rule, in accordance with Draft Conclusion 13; ILC 'Draft Conclusions on CIL Identification' (n 14) Draft Conclusion 13.

domestic practice, one final issue needs to be addressed. Sometimes, CIL interpretation is used to refer also to the 'interpretation' of the State practice (or of both elements).[71] First, this is not an argument against the interpretability of CIL, if anything this is an argument in favour of it, as it suggests that interpretation is ubiquitous in all the stages of law-ascertainment and content-determination of CIL.[72] However, the author feels compelled to raise some points with respect to 'interpretation of State practice'. If one by that refers to the assessment of whether there is sufficient, widespread, representative, consistent and virtually uniform practice, or the manner in which such practice is selected and the *gravitas* awarded to it, then indeed one could use the term 'interpretation of State practice', although in this author's view the more appropriate one would be 'evaluation', 'qualification' or 'assessment', to distinguish it properly from legal interpretation.[73] However, if one includes in that tools that are well established in legal interpretation, such as teleology, systemic integration etc,

71 See Sur, who clearly distinguishes between the *interpretation of the practice leading to the establishment of a customary rule*, on the one hand, and *the interpretation of the already established rule*, on the other hand; S Sur, *L'interprétation en droit international public* (LGDJ 1974) 189–90. Authors who approach CIL interpretation mainly from the angle of interpretation of State practice are: VP Tzevelekos, '*Juris dicere*: Custom as a Matrix, Custom as a Norm, and the Role of Judges and (their) Ideology in Custom Making' in N Rajkovic, TE Aalberts and Th Gammeltoft-Hansen (eds), The Power of Legality: Practices of International Law and their Politics (CUP 2016) 188; O Chasapis Tassinis, 'Customary International Law: Interpretation from Beginning to End' (2020) 31(1) EJIL 235; M Wood and O Sender, 'Between Theory, Practice, and "Interpretation" of Customary International Law' (*CIL Dialogues*, November 2022) <https://cil.nus.edu.sg/blogs/between-theory-practice-and-interpretation-of-customary-international-law/> last accessed 1 October 2023; see also J d' Aspremont, *The Discourse on Customary International Law* (OUP 2021).

72 'Law ascertainment' is understood as the identification of the legal act, while 'content-determination' as the identification of its content or meaning; in more detail J d' Aspremont, 'The Multidimensional Process of Interpretation: Content-Determination and Law-Ascertainment Distinguished' in A Bianchi, D Peat and M Windsor (eds), *Interpretation in International Law* (CUP 2015) 112.

73 Merkouris (n 21) Ch 4; see also Judge Charlesworth, who uses the terms '[e]valuting practice'; *Question of the Delimitation of the Continental Shelf between Nicaragua and Colombia beyond 200 nautical miles from the Nicaraguan Coast* (*Nicaragua v. Colombia*) ICJ (Judgment of 13 July 2023, Dissenting Opinion of Judge Charlesworth) <https://www.icj-cij.org/sites/default/files/case-related/154/154-20230713-jud-01-00-en.pdf> heading of Section II.F.2, last accessed 1 October 2023 (hereinafter *Delimitation of the Continental Shelf between Nicaragua and Colombia beyond 200 Nautical Miles*); see also M Fortuna, 'Different Strings of the Same Harp: Interpretation of Customary International Rules, their Identification and Treaty Interpretation' in P Merkouris, J Kammerhofer and N Arajärvi (eds), *The Theory, Practice and Interpretation of Customary International Law* (CUP 2022) 393; similarly Ryngaert who talks about 'evidentiary interpretation' and considers this as a false positive; C Ryngaert, 'Customary International Law Interpretation: The Role of Domestic

then we have left the realm of evaluating State practice, the 'pre-interpretative stage' as Dworkin would call it,[74] and entered into that of legal interpretation proper. The reason is quite simple. Let us take, for example, teleology. Can teleology be truly relevant in the interpretation of State practice in its proper sense? Of what is the *telos* that the judge is looking for? Is it the *telos* of State practice or the *telos* of an alleged rule?[75] If the latter, then we are clearly in the realm of interpretation of a CIL rule, and not of practice. So then, the only option left is that the judge is examining the *telos* of State practice. Here two are the potential scenarios: i) that the judge is examining the telos of a particular instance of State practice; or ii) the judge is examining the *telos* of the wider set of relevant practice. In scenario (i) that still does not help. The *telos* found and applied is that of a singular instance of practice. It is not a given that this same *telos* is shared by all other instances of State practice, or that even that it can be extrapolated to such a degree. Unavoidably, the judge would have to repeat the process when all relevant examples of State practice are taken into account. Which inexorably leads us to scenario (ii). But even here, the judge is not interpreting a collection of instances of State practice, but rather State practice as a reflection of a presumed or alleged CIL rule.[76] Without this postulate it is impossible to search for the *telos*. The judge is not looking for the *telos* of the practice, but rather the *telos* of a rule. Although this may not always be put in writing in judgments, the judges, when referring to teleology refer to teleology of a CIL rule, not of mere State practice. Even if they have not affirmatively established the existence of a CIL rule, they will always have a virtual representation of a CIL rule, a 'virtual Urtext'[77] the validity and limits of which they will test against its *telos*, 'normative environment' and potential limits (such as

Courts' in P Merkouris, J Kammerhofer and N Arajärvi (eds), *The Theory, Practice and Interpretation of Customary International Law* (CUP 2022) 481, 489–92.

74 DB Hollis, 'Sources in Interpretation Theories: An Interdependent Relationship' in S Besson and J d' Aspremont (eds), *The Oxford Handbook on the Sources of International Law* (OUP 2017) 422.

75 There could be instances where these two overlap or even coincide, but just because they do does not mean they are the same thing. Furthermore, when interpreting one looks at the telos of the rule and not the telos of each and every instance of State practice.

76 Even if one attempts to argue that these two coincide or overlap, again they are not the same thing. The reason for such presumed coincidence/overlap, as explained in the paragraph of the main text, is that the interpreter/judge in taking into account the *telos* of the whole State practice, is essentially looking at the *telos* of the rule. Unless the interpreter/judge has come to the conclusion that this is a rule, then they cannot properly assess the *telos* of the practice, as it may simply be *usus*. In that latter case, ie of only dealing with *usus* and not a binding legal rule, then this would and should take the analysis in a completely different direction.

77 To borrow Allot's terminology; Allot (n 21) 386.

jus cogens). Consequently, to say that in such cases what we are dealing with is 'interpretation of State practice' is rather a misnomer.

It is unsurprising, that even though Draft Conclusion 3 of the ILC Draft Conclusions on CIL Identification seems to suggest that 'interpretation of State practice' may be involved in the assessment of the existence of a rule of CIL, all the examples cited refer to the *telos* or system of a rule, not its practice, thus, demonstrating that what is actually occurring is interpretation of a postulated CIL rule, and not of just State practice.[78]

3 The Interpretability and Interpretation of Customary International Law in International Case-Law

In the previous Section we saw that despite its unwritten nature, not only is CIL interpretable from a theoretical point of view, but also that other non-written acts and instruments can and have been interpreted. However, although the theoretical validity of the interpretability of CIL is in and of itself of value, its import would be greatly enhanced if supported by relevant practice. In this and the following Sections it is to this that we shall turn our attention, namely examine whether CIL is not only interpretable but also interpreted.

Case-law would seem to be the first logical choice and, indeed, the majority of our analysis will focus on it. However, *indicia* of the recognition of the interpretability of CIL can also be found in Statutes of international courts and tribunals. Article 21 of the Rome Statute,[79] for instance, is one such example. This Article defines the law that the International Criminal Court (ICC) can apply, treaties, CIL and general principles. Not only is there no indication given that these sources should be or are treated differently, but also Article 21(2) explicitly notes that '[t]he [ICC] may apply *principles and rules of law as interpreted in its previous decisions*' (emphasis added). The ICC has consistently followed this language, often referring to principles and rules as having been interpreted in the ICC's previous judgments.[80] Article 21(3) reinforces this uniform approach towards all sources, as it simply refers to '[t]he *application and interpretation of law pursuant to this article*' (emphasis added), without indicating that rules may be treated differently depending on the source from which they have emerged.

---

78 ILC 'Draft Conclusions on CIL Identification' (n 14) Commentary to Draft Conclusion 3 [3] note 682.

79 1998 Rome Statute of the International Criminal Court (adopted 17 July 1998, entered into force 1 July 2002) 2187 UNTS 3 (hereinafter ICC Statute).

80 *Prosecutor v Jean-Pierre Bemba Gombo* (Fourth Decision on Victims' Participation of 12 December 2006) ICC Pre-Trial Chamber III, ICC-01/05-01/08-320 [15].

Naturally, one could argue that interpretation is used in this context in a sense different from that of legal interpretation as a content-determinative process. However, not only would that be somewhat counter-intuitive and bizarre especially in a legal text establishing an international court, but also the burden of proof would be on the side claiming such a 'special meaning'.

A perhaps clearer example can be traced to the Statutes of the International Court of Justice (ICJ) and of the Permanent Court of International Justice (PCIJ). Article 36 of the ICJ Statute, which is a near *verbatim* reproduction of the same article in the PCIJ Statute, regulates the jurisdiction of the Court in all legal disputes concerning 'a. the interpretation of a treaty' and 'b. any question of international law'. But where is the reference to interpretation of CIL? In fact, shouldn't the mere fact of the intentional switch in the language, with interpretation being used only for treaties while for custom the terms used are 'question of international law' argue in favour of a differential treatment between the two sources? *Prima facie* that would be a reasonable assumption. However, a foray into the preparatory work of the PCIJ Statute, indicates that this was not the intention of its drafters, the Advisory Committee of Jurists.

The language of what is now Article 36 was based on a draft proposed by Lord Phillimore.[81] While discussing this draft, the issue of interpretability of CIL was raised by another member of the Advisory Committee of Jurists, Ricci-Busatti. He suggested that the linguistic divergence between Article 36(a) and (b) was problematic. In order to resolve this, he proposed an alternate version which read 'a. the interpretation or application of a treaty; b. *the interpretation or application of a general rule of international law*'.[82] The substance of the amendment, ie the interpretability of CIL, did not meet with any objections. On the contrary, de la Pradelle and Hagerup were very critical of the flaws in Lord Phillimore's proposal, and lent their voice in support of Ricci-Busatti's proposal.[83] So why is it Lord Philimore's and not Ricci-Busatti's version that found its way in the final text of the PCIJ Statute? The reason had nothing to with whether CIL is interpretable or not. As mundane and technocratic as it may sound the reason was to ensure linguistic continuity. The terms used were a direct reproduction from Article 13 of the Covenant of the League of Nations and other earlier treaties, and the drafters felt the need that the same expression be retained.[84] As unfortunate as this may be, this does not detract from the

81 Advisory Committee of Jurists, *Procès Verbaux of the Meetings of the Advisory Committee of Jurists: 16 June–24 July 1920 with Annexes* (van Langenhuysen 1920) 252.

82 Ibid 265 and 275 (emphasis added).

83 Ibid 283–4.

84 Ibid 264–5 and 283–4.

fact that the interpretability of CIL was not only discussed during the *travaux préparatoires* of the PCIJ Statute but also a draft proposal of Article 36 was submitted that explicitly recognised such interpretability.

It is not only in Statutes and preparatory work that one can find traces of the interpretability of CIL. International courts and tribunals have, on occasion, explicitly recognised[85] it even in landmark cases. In the *Nicaragua* case, the ICJ held that '[r]ules which are identical in treaty law and in customary international law are also distinguishable by reference to the methods of interpretation and application'.[86] This would seem to imply that not only CIL is interpretable but also that there are, naturally, differences as to the methods of interpretation that apply to each. This is not surprising. As has already been shown with respect to interpretation of other non-treaty based rules,[87] this *mutatis mutandis* approach, which takes into account the special traits of the acts/rules in question seems to be the standard approach. Similarly, the ICJ has referred to the interpretability of CIL and general principles in a number of other cases, such as in *Barcelona Traction*,[88] and *Continental Shelf (Tunisia v Libya)*.[89] In the latter, the Court held that the consideration of the CIL rules 'may lead to widely differing results according to the way in which those principles and rules *are interpreted* and applied' and later on that 'the term "equitable

---

85 In some cases they have hinted at it, see, for instance, *Dispute over the Status and Use of the Waters of the Silala (Chile v. Bolivia)* [2022] ICJ Rep 614 [113]. However, for the purposes of this study the main focus will be on cases where there has been either explicit recognition or significant analysis that allows for the drawing of conclusions.

86 *Nicaragua* case (n 29) [178]. It is, of course, possible that one can read this sentence as supporting the view that it is meant to suggest that the distinction between CIL rules and treaty rules is in the form that the latter allow for interpretation, whereas the former does not (see Pomson, who adopts such a reading of the *Nicaragua* case; O Pomson, 'Methodology of Identifying Customary International Law Applicable to Cyber Activities' (2023) 36 LJIL 1023, 1034–5). However, there are two main objections to such a reading. Firstly, the structure of the sentence does not seem to support this. The distinction refers to the methods of interpretation and application, ie that those methods are different depending on whether the rule is a treaty rule or a CIL rule, not non-existent. If non-existence was the aim of the sentence then a different structure would have been appropriate to convey that message. Second, as is shown both in this Section and the ones that follow, the jurisprudence of the ICJ and of other international and domestic courts put this quote in context, as in those cases explicit reference is made to teleology, *effet utile*, evolutive interpretation etc. Thus, the language used is not one for determining whether a rules exists or not, but rather one for interpreting the rule and using the commonly known methods of interpretation.

87 See Section 2 above and the analysis therein on interpretation of unilateral acts.

88 *Barcelona Traction, Light and Power Company Limited (New Application: 1962) (Second Phase) (Belgium v Spain)* (Merits) [1970] ICJ Rep 3, Separate Opinion of Judge Tanaka [17], [101] and [105].

89 *Continental Shelf (Tunisia v Libyan Arab Jamahiriya)* (Judgment) [1982] ICJ Rep 18.

principles" *cannot be interpreted in the abstract*; it refers back to the principles and rules which may be appropriate in order to achieve an equitable result'.[90] This last part is also a nod to systemic integration, which will be analysed further below. In *Gulf of Maine* as well, the ICJ seems to lean in favour of interpreting CIL, by highlighting the drawbacks inherent in the nature of CIL. '*A body of detailed rules is not to be looked for in customary international law* … It is therefore unrewarding, *especially in a new and still unconsolidated field* like that involving the quite recent extension of the claims of States to areas which were until yesterday zones of the high seas, to look to general international law to provide a readymade set of rules that can be used for solving any delimitation problems that arise. *A more useful course is to seek a better formulation of the fundamental norm* on which the Parties were fortunate enough to be agreed, and whose existence in the legal convictions not only of the Parties to the present dispute, but of all States, is apparent from an examination of the realities of international legal relations'.[91] More recently, and in a different context, in the *Hadžihasanović* case, Judge Shahabuddeen also very clearly sided with the side of interpretability of CIL. 'If State practice and *opinio juris* have thrown up a relevant principle of customary international law, the solution turns on the principle. *But that does not bar all forward movement: a principle may need to be interpreted before it is applied.* … In the process of clarification, the Tribunal has the competence, which any court of law inevitably has, *to interpret an established principle of law and to consider whether, as so interpreted, the principle applies to the particular situation before it*'.[92]

Surprisingly, one of the most unreserved recognitions of the interpretability of CIL can be found in the *North Sea Continental Shelf* cases, which is considered as the *locus classicus* for the two-element approach to CIL. There Judge Tanaka not only recognised the interpretability of CIL, but identified two of its, in his view, key methods. 'Customary law, being vague and containing gaps compared with written law, requires precision and completion about its content. This task, in its nature being interpretative, would be incumbent upon the Court. *The method of logical and teleological interpretation can be applied in the case of customary law as in the case of written law*'.[93]

90 Ibid [38] and [70].

91 *Gulf of Maine* (n 53) [111] (emphasis added).

92 *Prosecutor v Enver Hadžihasanović, Mehmed Alagić and Amir Kubura* (Decision on Interlocutory Appeal Challenging Jurisdiction in Relation to Command Responsibility of 16 July 2003) ICTY Appeals Chamber, Case No IT-01-47-AR72, Partial Dissenting Opinion of Judge Shahabuddeen [9–10] (hereinafter *Hadžihasanović*) (emphasis added); similarly see ibid, Dissenting Opinion of Judge Hunter [10] and [39–40].

93 *North Sea Continental Shelf* (n 9) Dissenting Opinion of Judge Tanaka, 181 (emphasis added). In the same vein, see also ibid, Dissenting Opinion of Judge Morelli, 200. The

Before proceeding with examining the specific methods of CIL interpretation that international courts and tribunals have employed, the previous quote by Judge Tanaka needs to be addressed. It is unclear whether Judge Tanaka considered these two methods as clearly distinguishable, overlapping or entirely interchangeable. The use of the disjunctive 'or' would be an indicator against the complete interchangeability. Teleological interpretation is something that everyone is familiar with from treaty interpretation, and included in Article 31 VCLT. But what of logical interpretation? Despite the fact that with respect to treaty interpretation this does not appear *eo ipso* in the text of Article 31 VCLT, the term is not an entirely unknown quantity in international law. It was often used in pre-VCLT jurisprudence and the early codification attempts of the law of treaties. Perhaps the most pertinent of these is *Fiore's Draft Code* where it was suggested that treaty interpretation could be either *grammatical* or *logical*. According to this distinction logical interpretation included interpretative methods such as, intention of the parties, context, *contra proferentem*, equity, *ut res magis valeat quam pereat*, systemic/harmonious interpretation, and even teleology.[94] Of course, the content of logical interpretation as defined in *Fiore's Draft Code* is by no means set in stone, and was coloured by its juxtaposition to grammatical/textual interpretation. It would also seem that the use of the 'or' conjunction by Tanaka suggests that he was working under a somewhat different understanding of logical interpretation. This is even more so since in the case of CIL, grammatical interpretation *stricto sensu* is not possible.[95] However, what can be taken from this is that logical interpretation functions as an 'umbrella term' which covers several interpretative methods that everybody is familiar with, some of which have been incorporated in the text of the VCLT, while others have not although they are still being resorted to by international courts.[96] For this reason, is the potential overlap of 'logical interpretation' with a plethora of other more well-known interpretative approaches, and also because the purpose of this contribution is to demonstrate that CIL can and has

reference to gaps, and the idea of CIL interpretation as such a gap-filler is very reminiscent of Barile's writings; Barile (n 21); G Barile, 'La structure de l' ordre juridique international: règles générales et règles conventionnelles' (1978/III) 161 RdC 9, 61–2 and 85–7; G Barile, 'Il metodo logico-storico di rilevazione del diritto internazionale non scritto e le sue radici giusnaturalistiche' (1989) 72 Rivista di diritto internazionale 7, 21–4.

94 JW Garner, 'Codification of International Law: Part III – Law of Treaties – Appendix 4: Fiore's Draft Code' (1935) 29 AJIL Supp 1212, 1218–9.

95 Although as shall be seen below, courts tend to use a 'by proxy' version of it.

96 On a detailed presentation of the use of such methods, maxims and canons see J Klingler, Y Parkhomenko and C Salonidis (eds), *Between the Lines of the Vienna Convention? Canons and Other Principles of Interpretation in Public International Law* (Wolters Kluwer 2018).

been interpreted in international and domestic case-law, I will not take a firm position on the exact content of logical interpretation in the analysis below. However, when considerations regarding logical interpretation seem to be of import, then they will be addressed as they arise in the course of our analysis.

As was analysed in Section 2, one of the main arguments against the interpretability of CIL was the lack of text. Although, this argument was proven to not hold water, one would, nonetheless, still expect grammatical/textual interpretation to not be relevant. The reality is more of a sibyllic 'yes and no'. As Alland pointed out although CIL is unwritten it is always shrouded in a 'lexical garment'. It is this 'lexical garment' that international courts and tribunals often use as a substitute for a text. What is often the case, courts refer to documents that are allegedly reflective of CIL.[97] This in and of itself is not problematic, however, this is also often accompanied by textual and contextual interpretation on the basis of the specific language adopted in those documents, both in provisions that are reflective of CIL and in those that are not, which raises methodological concerns. A few characteristic examples that highlight this practice and issues: In *EC-Biotech*, the WTO Panel when interpreting the customary rules on interpretation, relied heavily on the text and context of the VCLT.[98] Of note is that several of the parties to the dispute were not parties to the VCLT.[99] In *Gulf of Maine* Judge Gros was of the opinion that '[t]he Court had … revised the 1969 Judgment so far as delimitation of the continental shelf was concerned, *by interpreting customary law in accordance with the known provisions of the draft convention produced by the Third United Nations Conference*'.[100] Again here the text used belonged to a document that was still at a draft stage. Finally, in *Tulip*, the investment Tribunal in order to determine whether the acts of a company owned predominantly by a State agency was attributable to Turkey, referred to the ILC Articles on State Responsibility (ARSIWA)[101] as a codification of CIL.[102] In fact, it relied so much on the text of the ARSIWA that its interpretation of the CIL rule on attribution revolves around the linguistic and syntactical choices

97 See also Allot's note that in the case of CIL, judges treat the *Untext* into a virtual *Urtext*; Allot (n 21) 386, and more generally 382–4.

98 *European Communities – Measures Affecting the Approval and Marketing of Biotech Products – Report of the Panel* (21 November 2006) WT/DS291/R 847, WT/DS292/R and WT/DS293/R [2006/III] DSR 847 [7.68–7.72] (hereinafter *EC-Biotech*).

99 The *EC-Biotech* case and its methodological *faux pas* are analysed in more detail below in Section 9.1.

100 *Gulf of Maine* (n 53) Dissenting Opinion of Judge Gros [8].

101 ILC, 'Draft Articles on Responsibility of States for Internationally Wrongful Acts with Commentaries' (23 April–1 June and 2 July–10 August 2001) UN Doc A/56/10, reproduced in [2001/II – Part Two] YBILC 31 (hereinafter ARSIWA).

102 *Tulip v Turkey* (Award of 10 March 2014) ICSID Case No ARB/11/28 [281].

of Article 8. According to the Tribunal, '[p]lainly, the words "instructions", "direction" and "control" are to be read disjunctively'.[103] It further buttressed this interpretation by reference to the ILC's Commentary.[104] The fact that the Tribunal engaged in an interpretation of CIL was also acknowledged in the subsequent annulment decision, where the committee clarified that 'the tribunal, in *interpreting* Article 8, took into account the ILC Commentary' and found that the tribunal ' correctly *interpreted* Article 8'.[105,106]

Most recently the ICJ, in *Question of the Delimitation of the Continental Shelf between Nicaragua and Colombia beyond 200 Nautical Miles from the Nicaraguan Coast*, muddled the identification and interpretation processes. It tried to identify relevant State practice and *opinio juris*, but also, although without explicitly stating so, interpreted the CIL rule enshrined in Article 76(1) of the 1982 United Convention on the Law of the Sea (UNCLOS).[107] In doing so, it relied on the text of provisions constituting the context of that provision, mainly Article 82(1) and Article 76(4)–(9) UNCLOS,[108] which, however, are of a debatable customary nature. Although such 'by proxy' textual interpretation is not uncommon, it needs to be exercised with great care to avoid overstepping the limits of the rule on interpretation[109] as happened in this case. The fact that this was an issue of interpretation of a CIL rule was rightly pointed out, and the lack of methodological rigour on the Court's part heavily criticised in Judge Charlesworth's dissenting opinion.[110]

---

103 Ibid [303].

104 Ibid [306] citing ARSIWA (n 101) Commentary to Art 8 [6].

105 *Tulip v Turkey* (Decision on Annulment of 30 December 2015) ICSID Case No ARB/11/28 [187–8] (emphasis added).

106 For a more detailed analysis of *Tulip* and other investment cases interpreting the customary rules on State responsibility see S Lekkas, 'The Uses of the Work of the International Law Commission on State Responsibility in International Investment Arbitration' in P Merkouris, A Kulick, JM Alvarez-Zarate and M Zenkiewicj (eds), *Custom and its Interpretation in International Investment Law* (CUP 2022) 93.

107 1982 United Nations Convention on the Law of the Sea (adopted 10 December 1982; entered into force 16 November 1994) 1833 UNTS 3 (hereinafter UNCLOS).

108 *Delimitation of the Continental Shelf between Nicaragua and Colombia beyond 200 Nautical Miles* (n 73) <https://www.icj-cij.org/sites/default/files/case-related/154/154-20230713-jud-01-00-en.pdf> [46–79] last accessed 1 October 2023.

109 See following paragraph and Section 9; see also TRICI-Law Guiding Principles (n 62) Guiding Principles 9 and 10, and accompanying Commentaries.

110 *Delimitation of the Continental Shelf between Nicaragua and Colombia beyond 200 Nautical Miles* (n 73) Dissenting Opinion of Judge Charlesworth [11–23]. For further criticisms regarding the Court's approach in the Judgment see also *Delimitation of the Continental Shelf between Nicaragua and Colombia beyond 200 Nautical Miles* (n 73) Dissenting

As can be seen from the above examples, international courts and tribunals tend to compensate for the lack of text of CIL rules, by using codificatory documents as a substitute. These documents can be either binding treaties (although sometimes not binding on some or all the parties to the dispute as in the case of *EC-Biotech* and *Delimitation of the Continental Shelf between Nicaragua and Colombia beyond 200 nautical miles*) or non-binding documents (draft Convention on the Law of the Sea in *Gulf of Maine* and ARSIWA in *Tulip*). Evidently, this practice cannot qualify as textual interpretation *stricto sensu*. What it actually resembles is more an application of the 'principle of systemic integration' as enshrined in Article 31(3)(c) VCLT, albeit in some cases in a more extended fashion, and/or *in pari materia* interpretation.[111] Since the latter overlaps with the principle of systemic integration and Article 32 VCLT, this would be the more methodologically consistent categorisation of this type of 'by proxy' textual interpretation.

Reference to codification instruments is far from the only tool in the interpretative arsenal of international judges when interpreting CIL. Another, and perhaps most often utilised, method is the teleological one. Judge Tanaka's explicit reference to teleological interpretation of CIL in *North Sea Continental Shelf* has already been mentioned. However, there is a veritable cornucopia of international cases that have resorted to this interpretative method for CIL. Investment tribunals, for instance have on several occasions declared that the purpose of an award of interest under Article 38 ARSIWA is to 'ensure full reparation'. Given this they then proceed to award compound interest despite the fact that both ARSIWA is silent on the matter and its Commentary seems to be leaning in a different direction.[112] Often in these pronouncements there is a

---

Opinion of Judge Tomka <https://www.icj-cij.org/sites/default/files/case-related/154/154-20230713-jud-01-01-en.pdf> last accessed 1 October 2023.

111 On *in pari materia* interpretation see PF Henin, '*In Pari Materia* Interpretation in J Klingler, Y Parkhomenko and C Salonidis (eds), *Between the Lines of the Vienna Convention? Canons and Other Principles of Interpretation in Public International Law* (Wolters Kluwer 2018) 211.

112 Indicatively, *Quiborax v Bolivia* (Award of 16 September 2015) ICSID Case No ARB/06/2 [514] and [520–4]; *Crystallex v Venezuela* (Award of 4 April 2016) ICSID Case No ARB(AF)/11/2 [932] and [935]. For a detailed discussion on the issue of ARSIWA, reparations and CIL interpretation see Lekkas (n 106) and E Giakoumakis, 'A Riddle Wrapped in a Mystery Inside an Enigma: Equitable Considerations in the Assessment of Damages by Investment Tribunals' in P Merkouris, A Kulick, JM Alvarez-Zarate and M Zenkiewicj (eds), *Custom and its Interpretation in International Investment Law* (CUP 2024) 179.

combination of various methods, eg teleology with 'by proxy' textual interpretation of CIL.[113]

International criminal tribunals have also often referred to the object and purpose of a CIL in the process of interpreting it. Sometimes also reference is made to its nature, which may not necessarily be the exact same thing but for reason of simplicity this will also be mentioned here. In *Čelebići* the Trial Chamber had this mythological reference to make with respect to CIL interpretation. 'The international community can only come to grips with the *hydra-headed elusiveness* of human conduct *through a reasonable as well as a purposive interpretation of existing provisions of international customary law*'.[114] Reasonable and purposive seem here to be used as substitutes for Tanaka's logical and teleological interpretation, although an argument could also be made that the choice of 'reasonable' alludes to the use of terms such as '*ratio*' and '*rationale*', which are also often encountered in international and domestic case-law.[115] These thoughts aside, the writing on the wall is clear, namely that teleological interpretation is a method central to the interpretative exercise of CIL.

To further substantiate this point; in *Hadžihasanović*, Judge Shahabuddeen resorted to the object and purpose of command responsibility in order to determine whether it could be applied in the case of a change in command.[116] Notably he also referred to 'intent' as well, but that seems to have been used as a place-holder term alluding to the *telos* of the rule.[117,118] In *Orić*, Judge Daqun Liu based his Partially Dissenting Opinion and Declaration on the purpose of command responsibility, which was to 'to ensure compliance with the laws and customs of war and international humanitarian law generally'.[119] He followed that up a few paragraphs below by referring to the 'nature of command responsibility' in order to conclude that the correct interpretation of the CIL rule on

113 Lekkas (n 106).

114 *Prosecutor v Delalić et al* (Judgment of 16 November 1998) ICTY Trial Chamber, Case No IT-96-21-T [170] (hereinafter *Čelebići*).

115 Whether these should be considered as completely separate from teleology is beyond the scope of this contribution. For the use of these terms in domestic cases, and some additional thoughts see also Section 4.

116 *Hadžihasanović* (n 92) Partial Dissenting Opinion of Judge Shahabuddeen [9–10].

117 Ibid [10]; 'In acting accordingly, the Appeals Chamber will not be changing customary international law but will be carrying out *its true intent by interpreting and applying one of its existing principles*' (emphasis added).

118 For a detailed analysis of *Hadžihasanović* and similar cases, see Fortuna (n 73) and M Fortuna, *Interpretation of Customary International Law in International Courts* (University of Groningen, 2023).

119 *Prosecutor v Naser Orić* (Judgment of 3 July 2008) ICTY Appeals Chamber, Case No IT-03-68-A, Partially Dissenting Opinion and Declaration of Judge Daqun Liu [30].

command responsibility does not support a distinction before and after a commander assumes command.[120]

Although not an international court, the ILC has as well in its recent work on immunities characterised the teleological interpretation of the CIL rules on immunities as 'necessary' and leading to 'more nuanced conclusions',[121] so much so, in fact that teleological interpretation acts as an interpretative limit. '*The determination of [the immunity's] scope and its interpretation must remain within the limits defined by the ends sought*. In particular, it can be invoked only in the interest of the State whose sovereign equality it claims to preserve, and only for the purpose of safeguarding legitimate rights and interests of the State that are protected under international law'.[122]

A final point with respect to teleological interpretation, is that international courts and tribunals sometimes do not base their interpretation on the *telos* or logic of the CIL rule in question, but rather of the entire area of law within which the CIL rule exists.[123] Such a *lato sensu* teleological interpretation borders on and potentially overlaps with systemic interpretation, to which I shall now focus the analysis.

The resort to the 'principle of systemic integration' has already been partly discussed earlier when examining the 'by proxy' textual interpretation. However, in addition to that, instances of more classical systemic interpretation are also peppered throughout international case-law. In such cases, international courts and tribunals refer to the 'normative environment' or 'normative

120 Ibid [32].

121 ILC 'Fifth Report' (n 18) [150].

122 Ibid [147(c)].

123 See, for instance: '[a] first ground on which the *Nicaragua* test as such may be held to be unconvincing is based *on the very logic of the entire system of international law on State responsibility*'; *Prosecutor v Duško Tadić* (Appeal Judgement of 15 July 1999) ICTY Appeals Chamber, Case No IT-94-1-A [116] and more generally [116–23]; '[i]t must next be noted that the "overall control" test has the major drawback of broadening the scope of State responsibility well beyond the *fundamental principle governing the law of international responsibility*'; *Application of the Convention on the Prevention and Punishment of the Crime of Genocide* (*Bosnia and Herzegovina v Serbia and Montenegro*) (Judgment) [2007] ICJ Rep 43 [406] (hereinafter *Application of the Genocide Convention*); 'primary object of interpretation' *Maritime Delimitation and Territorial Questions between Qatar and Bahrain* (*Qatar v Bahrain*) (Jurisdiction and Admissibility) [1995] ICJ Rep 6, Dissenting Opinion of Vice-President Schwebel 27; '[i]n this connection, *certain basic considerations inherent in the nature of the territorial sea*, bring to light certain criteria which, though not entirely precise, can provide courts with an adequate basis for their decisions, which can be adapted to the diverse facts in question' *Fisheries* (UK *v Norway*) (Judgment) [1951] ICJ Rep 116, 133 (emphasis added to all quotes in this note).

background' of the CIL rule being interpreted and which colours its content.[124] As the ICJ noted in the *Interpretation of the Agreement of 25 March 1951 between the WHO and Egypt* Advisory Opinion, 'a rule of international law, whether customary or conventional, *does not operate in a vacuum*; it operates in relation to facts and *in the context of a wider framework of legal rules of which it forms only a part*'.[125] Driving this point home from an interpretative and immunities angle, *Special Rapporteur* Hernández more recently and very precisely emphasised that this 'requires *that immunity be analysed not in isolation*, but in connection with the rest of the norms and institutions that make up the system ... [T]he immunity of State officials from foreign criminal jurisdiction, as a component of this system, *should be interpreted in a systemic fashion to ensure that this institution does not produce negative effects on, or nullify, other components of the contemporary system of international law understood as a whole*'.[126] This last part is a nod as well, to a variety of potentially logical interpretations such as *effet utile* and *ad absurdum* interpretations. Such a connection between systemic interpretation and *effet utile* or *ad absurdum* constructions can be noted in the entirely different context of investment law, in *Devas*,[127] and of international criminal law, in *Orić*.[128]

The strong presence of the 'principle of systemic integration' in case-law relating to CIL interpretation may be also attributable to the fact that before acknowledging the existence of a conflict between rules, international courts tend to attempt to harmonise the content of the rules through interpretation in 'dialectical terms',[129] a process which has been popularised as 'harmonisation through interpretation'.[130] Such a balanced interpretation of CIL can be clearly

---

124 *Continental Shelf* (*Tunisia v Libyan Arab Jamahiriya*) (Judgment) [182] ICJ Rep 18 [38] and [70], *Mondev International Ltd v USA*, (Award of 11 October 2002) ICSID Case No ARB(AF)/99/2 [127]; *Jurisdictional Immunities of the State* (*Germany v Italy: Greece intervening*) [2012] ICJ Rep 99 [57]; *Certain Activities carried out by Nicaragua in the Border Area and Construction of a Road in Costa Rica along the San Juan River* (*Nicaragua v Costa Rica*) [2015] ICJ Rep 665, Separate Opinion of Judge Donoghue [3–10].

125 *Interpretation of the Agreement of 25 March 1951 between the WHO and Egypt* (Advisory Opinion) [1980] ICJ Rep 73 [10] (emphasis added).

126 ILC 'Fifth Report' (n 18) [142] (emphasis added); see also ibid [175].

127 *Devas v India* (Decision on Jurisdiction and Merits of 25 July 2016) PCA Case No 2013–09 [278–80].

128 *Prosecutor v Naser Orić* (n 119) Partially Dissenting Opinion and Declaration of Judge Daqun Liu [30].

129 ILC 'Fifth Report' (n 18) [147(d)].

130 See ILC, 'Report on Fragmentation of International Law: Difficulties Arising from the Diversification and Expansion of International Law, Finalized by Martti Koskenniemi' (1 May–9 June and 3 July–11 August 2006) UN Doc A/CN.4/L.682 [37–43], [88], [229–31], [277] and [411]. On the VCLT rules on interpretation as a potential tool for harmonisation

seen, for instance, in the Separate Opinions of judges in the *Jurisdictional Immunities* case, where the need to ensure a balance among the various values and norms of the international legal system, namely immunities, on the one hand, and *jus cogens* violations, on the other hand were central to their judicial reasoning.[131]

Before closing this Section, and since *effet utile* and *ad absurdum* constructs were already mentioned, a few more interpretative methods that also show up, albeit not with the same frequency as the ones analysed above, but which also seem to fall under the umbrella-term of logical interpretation[132] would be those of *per analogiam* interpretations,[133] and interpretations by necessary implication.[134]

4 The Interpretability and Interpretation of Customary International Law in Domestic Case-Law[135]

CIL is not a unique trait of international law. Most domestic legal systems address domestic customary law as one of their sources. Naturally, there is no uniform approach as to the hierarchy of and restrictions on, often of a constitutional nature, domestic customary law and its application.[136] There is, however,

---

see F Zarbiyev, 'Les règles d'interprétation de la Convention de Vienne sur le droit des traités: un outil d'harmonisation en droit international?' in C Chappuis et al (eds), *L'harmonisation internationale du droit* (Schulthess 2007) 75.

131 *Jurisdictional Immunities of the State* (n 124), Separate Joint Opinion of Judges Higgins, Kooijmans and Buergenthal [51] and [71–9].

132 See Section 3 and discussion on Fiore's draft code and Tanaka's statement in *North Sea Continental Shelf.*

133 *Jurisdictional Immunities of the State* (n 124).

134 *EDF International SA, SAUR International SA and Leon Participaciones Argentinas SA v Argentine Republic* (Award of 11 June 2012), ICSID Case No ARB/03/23 [1171], [1177] and [1181]; *EDF International SA, SAUR International SA and Leon Participaciones Argentinas SA v Argentine Republic* (Annulment Decision of 5 February 2016) ICSID Case No ARB/03/23 [291] and [325]. On this method of interpretation, see AD Mitchell and T Voon, 'The Rule of Necessary Implication' in J Klingler, Y Parkhomenko and C Salonidis (eds), *Between the Lines of the Vienna Convention? Canons and Other Principles of Interpretation in Public International Law* (Wolters Kluwer 2018) 331.

135 The domestic cases cited in this study have been selected as highlighting key features of the methods of interpretation of CIL employed, while at the same time also satisfying concerns of both geographical and 'legal families' representativeness.

136 See eg, Art 2(4) of the Constitution of Kenya (2010 amendment) <http://www.parliament.go.ke/sites/default/files/2023-03/The_Constitution_of_Kenya_2010.pdf> last accessed 1 October 2023.

a tendency for domestic customary law to yield when it conflicts with written laws.

A slightly more nuanced example of this can be found in the hybrid legal system of Kenya.[137] Customary law is recognised in the Kenyan legal system by virtue of Section 3 of the Judicature Act.[138] Noteworthy is, however, Section 3(2), which imposes certain limitations to the applicability of customary law. According to this, customary law can be resorted to '... so far as it is applicable and *not repugnant to justice and morality* and is *not inconsistent with any written law*'.[139] Of import here is not only the issue of resolving a potential normative conflict in favour of written instruments, but also that any rule of customary law may not be 'repugnant to justice and morality'. This is known as the repugnancy clause,[140] and it is interesting as it, by necessity, opens up customary law to interpretation. Any such determination of repugnancy would undoubtedly entail an interpretative exercise, such as, for instance, the normative environment or the *telos* of the rule.[141]

Other legal systems, such as the Greek one, not only explicitly acknowledge the interpretability of customary law, but also make no distinction between domestic or international customary law. Article 559(1) of the Greek Code of Civil Procedure, for instance, provides that '[a]n appeal is allowed only 1) if a rule of substantive law has been violated, which includes the rules of interpretation of legal acts, *regardless of whether this entails a law or custom*, Greek or

---

137 Hybrid, in these sense that it cannot be categorized as strictly monist or dualist.

138 Judicature Act (2012 rev edn) <http://kenyalaw.org/kl/fileadmin/pdfdownloads/Acts/JudicatureAct_Cap8.pdf> last accessed 1 October 2023.

139 Emphasis added.

140 The landmark case in Kenya is the *R v Amkeyo* [1917] EALR 14. See in more detail, Kenya National Research Team, 'Report on Interpretation of Customary Law in Kenya' (*TRICI-Law*, 2022) <https://tricilawofficial.wordpress.com/wp-content/uploads/2022/02/kenya-final-report_2022.pdf> last accessed 1 October 2023.

141 See, for instance, *Katet Nchoe and another v Republic of Kenya* where Judge Emukule had this to say regarding the custom of female genital mutilation: 'It is the justice of all the surrounding circumstances of the custom in point. There is no more justice in this custom if ever there was any. I doubt there was any morality in it ... The Repugnancy Clause has been defined in the Ghanaian Constitution to mean no more than a custom that is harmful to the physical and social well-being of the citizen. In our case, female genital mutilation is certainly harmful to the physical and no doubt the psychological and sound well being of the victim. It may lead to child-birth complications, in this case, it led to premature death of a teenager. That kind of custom could be truly be well discarded and buried in the annuals of history, just as we no longer remove our two, four or six teeth from our lower jaws, or adorn our faces, cheeks with healed blisters'; *Katet Nchoe and another v Republic of Kenya* (11 February 2011) High Court of Kenya [2011] eKLR <http://kenyalaw.org/caselaw/cases/view/74018/> last accessed 1 October 2023.

foreign, of domestic or international law'.[142] This has been interpreted by the Supreme Civil and Criminal Court of Greece in the following manner: 'The legal rule is violated, if it is not applied, … as well as if it is applied incorrectly …, *and the violation is manifested either by false interpretation* [*misinterpretation*] or by incorrect application'.[143] Neither the Greek Code of Civil Procedure nor the relevant jurisprudence differentiate in their approach on the basis either of the source or the (non-)international nature of the rule.[144]

Although domestic legal systems can furnish us with examples of interpretation of domestic customary law, since the focus of this contribution is on CIL, it is to such examples drawn from domestic case-law that this study will turn to now. The interpretability of CIL in domestic courts is reliant on a number of factors, eg on whether there are any constitutional restrictions[145] or on whether one is dealing with a monist or dualist State, or anything in between these two extremes of the spectrum.[146] The latter may be of relevance because these two correspond to different methods of reception of international law into the domestic legal system. Whereas monist States *incorporate* international law,[147] dualist States require a *transformation* act.[148] However, especially with respect to CIL this is further complicated as even States that are considered textbook dualist States, have a more nuanced approach as to what concerns rules of

142 Greek Code of Civil Procedure, ΦΕΚ A 182 19851024, Art 559(1) (author's translation and emphasis added).

143 *Judgment 7/2006* (23 February 2006) Areios Pagos, Greece, ΟΛ.ΑΠ 7/2006, referring also to *Judgment 4/2005* (21 April 2005) Areios Pagos, Greece, ΟΛ.ΑΠ 4/2005.

144 M Margaritis, 'Article 559' in K Kerameas, D Kondilis and N Nikas, *Interpretation of the Code of Civil Procedure, Vol I, Articles 1–590* (Sakkoulas 2000) 1000; Ch Apalagaki, *Code of Civil Procedure: Article by Article Interpretation, Articles 1–590* (4th edn, Nomiki Vivliothiki 2016) 1405–9.

145 Eg Art 10(1) of the Constitution of the Italian Republic (2020 amendment) <https://www.senato.it/documenti/repository/istituzione/costituzione_inglese.pdf> last accessed 1 October 2023.

146 On why this binary divide is not as airtight as one might think, and for a brief sketch of some of the possible variations, see ILA, 'Final Report of the Study Group on Principles on the Engagement of Domestic Courts with International Law: Mapping the Engagement of Domestic Courts with International Law' (*ILA*, 2016) [17–20] <https://www.ila-hq.org/en_GB/documents/conference-study-group-report-johannesburg-2016> last accessed 1 October 2023; see also the various accompanying State Reports.

147 See, for instance, Art 28(2) of the Constitution of Greece (2008 rev) <https://www.hellenicparliament.gr/UserFiles/f3c70a23-7696-49db-9148-f24dce6a27c8/001-156%20aggliko.pdf> last accessed 1 October 2023.

148 See, for instance, the UK.

this type. The UK, for instance, 'arguably "incorporates" customary law into the common law, or rather treats it as a source of the common law'.[149]

Despite such potential restrictions and variations, CIL has been interpreted in domestic legal systems as well, and the interpretative tools employed show remarkable similarities with those seen in international case-law. As mentioned in Section 3, so it must be repeated here, that the aim is not to provide an exhaustive list of all possible interpretative rules, but rather to highlight some key methods used that demonstrate that domestic courts as well interpret CIL.

In *Queen v Alqudsi* and *Sea Shepherd* the domestic courts referred to the text and definitions provided in both binding and non-binding instruments. In *Queen v Alqudsi* the Supreme Court of New South Wales focused on the text and *telos* of the 1970 Friendly Relations Declaration[150] in order to make a pronouncement on whether States had a duty not to acquiesce in conduct by persons within their own territories that was designed to lead to armed hostilities in other states. More specifically, the question was whether such a customary law obligation was restricted only to mercenaries or included a broader set of individuals. The Supreme Court did not examine State practice and *opinio juris* on the matter, but rather zeroed in on the text of the Friendly Relations Declaration. In its view, the Declaration 'did not distinguish between mercenaries …, on the one hand, and the broader genus of foreign fighters (motivated by religion, culture, ideology or some other reason), on the other. *The terms of the declaration and its purpose are inconsistent with any such distinction*'.[151] In essence, the Court used the Declaration (in its entirety) as both a linguistic and teleological proxy of the customary rule.

Similarly, in *Sea Shepherd*, where the issue at hand was whether environmental activists who had used aggressive tactics against whaling ships could be considered as pirates. The 9th Circuit Court of Appeals not only relied heavily on the precise wording of piracy in UNCLOS[152] and the High

149 ILA (n 146) [18]; For a detailed exposition of the curious position of customary international law in the legal system of the UK see R O' Keefe, 'The Doctrine of Incorporation Revisited' (2008) 79 BYIL 7; Similar approaches to the UK one have also emerged in States such as Canada, Israel, and South Africa; ILA (n 146) [18].

150 UN General Assembly, 'Declaration on Principles of International Law concerning Friendly Relations and Cooperation among States in Accordance with the Charter of the United Nations' (24 October 1970) UN Doc A/RES/25/2625.

151 *The Queen v Alqudsi* (Motion to Quash Indictment and Summons for Declaratory Relief of 27 August 2015) Supreme Court of New South Wales, Australia [2015] NSWSC 1222 [141–2] (emphasis added).

152 UNCLOS (n 107) Art 101.

Seas Convention,[153] but proceeded with an ordinary meaning analysis of the terms 'private ends', even using *Webster's New International Dictionary*.[154] As seen also in international case-law, despite the unwritten nature of CIL, courts tend to use documents (both binding and non-binding) which are allegedly reflective of CIL as a textual substitute, and then proceed with a 'by proxy' textual interpretation. As mentioned in Section 3 this could be seen as bearing similarities with a 'systemic integration' type of interpretation or *in pari materia* interpretation (depending on whether the text referred to is binding or not), but when it goes beyond that referring to the context of the document or even its preparatory work,[155] this may raise methodological concerns.

Another dominant pattern emerging from domestic case-law is reference to either the *telos* of the rule or its rationale. Whether the latter should be considered as part and parcel of a teleological interpretation or is somewhat more akin to logical interpretation, is quite subjective and may also vary depending on the context and the manner in which it is being used in each particular case. For the purposes of the present analysis and for reason of simplicity, both teleological and rationale-based interpretation will be examined as falling under the same pattern. Further down this Section, domestic cases where logical interpretation was explicitly indicated will be analysed separately.

In *Her Majesty the Queen in Right of Canada v Edelson and others* the respondents Rivka and Aaron Reinhold had leased a house in Herzliya to the applicant, Canada. This was meant to serve as the residence of the Canadian ambassador to Israel. The Canadian ambassador was granted the option of extending the lease for three additional periods, contingent on securing the consent of Bank Mizrahi, in whose name a mortgage on the house was registered. The mortgage was later transferred to Mr Edelson, and the Canadian government was informed that he withheld his consent as to the extension of the lease. The owners demanded that the Canadian government vacate the premises at the end of the original lease. The Canadian government refused, claiming that it had the option of extending the lease, and that in any event the domestic courts had no jurisdiction as this issue was covered by State immunity.[156] The Supreme Court of Israel was called to identify the content of the CIL rule on State immunity and the criteria to be used in distinguishing between *acta jure*

153 1958 Convention on the High Seas (adopted 29 April 1958, entered into force 30 September 1962) 450 UNTS 11.

154 *Institute of Cetacean Research v Sea Shepherd Conservation Society*, 725 F.3d 940 (9th Cir 2013) [5–6].

155 See, for instance, the analysis in Section 9.1 on the *EC-Biotech* case.

156 *Her Majesty the Queen in Right of Canada v Edelson and others* (3 June 1997) Supreme Court of Israel PLA 7092/94, 51(1) PD 625 [1].

imperii and *acta jure gestionis*. In order to achieve this the Supreme Court of Israel acknowledged first that this is an issue of content-determination,[157] and then that '[t]he difficulty in delineating the scope of restricted immunity stems from the lack of clarity surrounding the very rationale underlying the doctrine of State immunity. How can we define the parameters of the doctrine of State immunity if its underlying rationale is unknown?'.[158] It then proceeded to discredit various theories as to the rationale of the rule of State immunity. In the court's view neither *par in parem non habet imperium* nor the foreign State's independence and dignity were sufficient reasons for granting a State immunity. In fact, according to the domestic court, the rule of law, demanded the opposite.

The same issue, of distinguishing between *acta jure imperii* and *acta jure gestionis* arose in the *Former Consular Employee at the Consulate General of Croatia in Stuttgart v Croatia* case. A Croatian national, residing in Germany, had been employed in Consulate General of Croatia in Stuttgart. Despite a request from the employee to be enrolled under the German social security system, Croatia neglected to do this, and when a claim was brought by the employee against it invoked State immunity. The Higher Regional Court was very clear that the only way to qualify an act as either an *actum jure imperii* or an *actum jure gestionis* 'must be based on the sense and purpose of State immunity', thus again clearly indicating that the solution requires a teleological interpretation of the customary rule.[159] Similar views on State immunity were also expressed in the *'Comfort Women'*,[160] and *Ferrini* cases[161] but since they were also more strongly tied to logical interpretation and an *ut res magis valeat* construction

---

157 'This is not a simple undertaking by any means. Indeed, while it is one thing to reject the absolute application of immunity, it is quite another to determine restricted immunity's scope'; ibid [22].

158 Ibid [22].

159 *Former Consular Employee at the Consulate General of Croatia in Stuttgart v Croatia* (Second Instance Order of 23 October 2014) Higher Regional Court of Stuttgart, Case No 5 U 52/14, ILDC 2428 (DE 2014) [43] (author's translation). The original text goes: 'Ferner hat sich die Qualifikation der Handlung am Sinn und Zweck der staatlichen Immunität zu orientieren'.

160 *Case No 2016 Ga-Hap 505092* (8 January 2021) Central District Court of Seoul [3.C.3.6–3.C.3.7] <https://womenandwar.net/resources-eng/?q=YToxOntzOjEyOiJrZXl3b3JkX3R5cGUiO3M6MzoiYWxsIjt9&bmode=view&idx=18323479&t=board> (unofficial translation by Woohee Kim, The Korean Council for Justice and Remembrance for the Issues of Military Sexual Slavery by Japan) last accessed 1 October 2023 (hereinafter *'Comfort Women'* case).

161 *Ferrini v Germany* (Appeal Decision of 11 March 2004) Supreme Court of Cassation of Italy, Case No 5044/04 [9.2].

(in 'Comfort *Women*') and systemic integration (in *Ferrini*), they will be analysed in more detail further down this Section.

As mentioned above, Sur characterised the interpretation of CIL as 'negentropic', ie reducing entropy, 'because it constantly nourishes and updates it'.[162] Domestic courts seem to share this view, with several courts recognizing the dynamic/evolutive character of CIL, thus, naturally opening the door to evolutive interpretation.[163] This was explicitly stated in *Public Committee against Torture in Israel and Palestinian Society for the Protection of Human Rights and the Environment v Israel and others*. where the Israel Supreme Court was called to decide on whether the policy of 'targeted killings' by Israel of members of Palestinian terrorist organizations was legal under international law. The domestic court held that '[r]ules developed against the background of a reality which has changed *must take on dynamic interpretation which adapts them, in the framework of accepted interpretational rules, to the new reality ... In the spirit of such interpretation, we shall now proceed to the customary international law dealing with the status of civilians who constitute unlawful combatants*'.[164]

Perhaps together with teleological interpretation, the principle of systemic integration, whereby reference to the normative environment of the rule is made, seems to be one of the most utilised methods in the interpretative arsenal of domestic courts as far as CIL is concerned. Earlier we saw reference to other treaties and CIL as a substitute for 'textual interpretation'. However, this is not the only manner in which other rules are taken into account. There are several accounts where domestic courts have resorted to other rules in order to interpret CIL, in the traditional 'systemic integration' fashion.

Ferrini is a textbook example of this. Ferrini was an Italian, who during World War II was arrested and forced to work at a German munition factory, without being recognized the status of prisoner of war. More than four decades later

162 Sur 'La créativité' (n 22) 295.

163 *'Comfort Women'* case (n 160) [3.C.3.3]; *SRYYY v Minister for Immigration and Multicultural and Indigenous Affairs* (17 March 2005) Federal Court of Australia [2005] FCAFC 42 [47]. This is also true for domestic customary law; see, for instance, *Martha Wanjiru Kimata and another v Dorcas Wanjiru and another* (24 February 2015) High Court of Kenya [2015] eKLR, Civil Appeal No 94 of 2014 [14] <http://kenyalaw.org/caselaw/cases/view/106319/> last accessed 1 October 2023.

164 *Public Committee against Torture in Israel and Palestinian Society for the Protection of Human Rights and the Environment v Israel and others* (13 December 2006) Supreme Court of Israel, HCJ 769/02 [28]; see in more detail N Mileva, *A Theory of Interpretation for Customary International Law* (University of Groningen, 2023); N Mileva, 'The Role of Domestic Courts in the Interpretation of Customary International Law: How can we Learn from Domestic Interpretive Practices?' in P Merkouris, J Kammerhofer and N Arajärvi (eds), *The Theory, Practice and Interpretation of Customary International Law* (CUP 2022) 453.

he went in front of Italian courts claiming damages from the actions of the German troops. The Arezzo District Court, relying on Germany's State immunity, rejected the suit as did the Court of Appeals. However, the Italian Supreme Court of Cassation reversed these judgments finding that there is an exception to State immunity when the State has committed acts that are in violation of *jus cogens* norms.[165]

The Supreme Court of Cassation arrived at this conclusion by referring to the fact that respect for inviolable human rights had attained the status of a fundamental principle of the international legal system. The emergence of this principle, in the Court's view

> cannot but influence the scope of the other principles that traditionally inform this legal system, particularly that of the "sovereign equality" of States, which constitutes the rationale for the recognition of state immunity from foreign civil jurisdiction. *Indeed, legal rules should not be interpreted in isolation* since they complement and integrate each other, and the application of one is dependent on the others [see *Al-Adsani* and *McElhinney*]. These decisions make specific reference to conventional norms. *However, it is unquestionably true that similar criteria apply to the interpretation of customary norms, which like the others are part of a system and therefore may only be correctly understood in relation to other norms that form an integral part of the same legal system.*[166]

Several of the cases already mentioned also resort to the principle of systemic integration in order to ensure that any interpretation of CIL that they are considering has its finger on the pulse of the international community, is consistent with existing international obligations and contributes to the avoidance of normative conflict by virtue of 'harmonisation through interpretation'.[167]

165 This, of course, was not the end of the line. A case was brought before the ICJ by Germany, claiming that through these judgments Italy had failed to respect Germany's jurisdictional immunity. The ICJ interpreted customary international law and arrived at an interpretation according to which the recognition of jurisdictional immunity to Germany was not in conflict with *jus cogens* norms, as they functioned on different planes. Immunities were procedural in nature, whereas *jus cogens* norms were substantive, thus no conflict could emerge. As a result, the ICJ concluded that Italy had indeed violated Germany's jurisdictional immunity. In 2014, the Italian Constitutional Court was called to grapple with the aftermath of *the Jurisdictional Immunities* case and delivered its judgment in *Sentenza No 238/2014*.

166 *Ferrini v Germany* (n 161) [9.2] (emphasis added).

167 *Her Majesty the Queen in Right of Canada v Edelson and others* (n 156) [22]; *Attorney-General v Zaoui and Inspector-General of Intelligence and Security and Human Rights*

Logical interpretation also features prominently as an 'attractor' with respect to interpretation of CIL. As shown in Section 3 logical interpretation is somewhat of a mercurial concept and can act as an umbrella term under which various interpretative methods can fall. In the context of the present inquiry the most notable manifestations are those of *ad absurdum* constructions, which are also closely connected to *ut res magis valeat*/principle of effectiveness constructions, and *per analogiam* constructions.[168]

In the *'Comfort Women'* case, the South Korean District Court, like so many other cases already examined in this study had to tackle issues of State immunity but in the context of whether such immunity could be invoked for crimes against humanity committed during WWII. This case arose out of an action submitted by South Korean women, who had been forced into sexual slavery during World War II in what were known euphemistically as 'comfort stations'. From the late 1930s, Imperial Japan mobilized both men and women from the colonial Korean peninsula as 'Volunteer Labor Corps' for a variety of work. In the case in question, the applicants were mobilised to 'comfort stations', which had been first installed by the Japanese Navy as a preventive measure against the frequent rapes committed by Japanese soldiers during the 1932 Shanghai Incident, that resulted in local resistance and sexually transmitted diseases. Between 1931 and 1945, military 'comfort stations' were installed and operated in a number of Japanese-held territories and front lines, in Southeast Asia and the South Pacific area. As the Seoul District Court notes in its summary of the facts, '[i]mperial Japan mobilized "comfort women" to comfort stations installed in the battlefronts through various methods targeting women from various countries in its occupied territories, including its own country. The methods of mobilization included 1) forced mobilization through physical force, threats, and abduction of women, 2) mobilization through local community leaders, government officials, and schools, 3) mobilization through false promises of "employment and big money," 4) commission to private recruiters, and 5) mobilization through labor corps and conscription'.[169]

Commission (*intervening*) (21 June 2005) Supreme Court of New Zealand [2005] NZSC 38 [32–3]; *A v Swiss Federal Public Prosecutor* (25 July 2012) Swiss Federal Criminal Court, BB.2011.140 [5.4.3].

168 On the two faces of the principle of effectiveness (one avoiding rendering a provision meaningless, and the other being a more teleological and expansive approach to the scope of the provision) see C Braumann and A Reinisch, '*Effet Utile*' in J Klingler, Y Parkhomenko and C Salonidis (eds), *Between the Lines of the Vienna Convention? Canons and Other Principles of Interpretation in Public International Law* (Wolters Kluwer 2018) 47.

169 *'Comfort Women'* case (n 160) [1.B.1.a–1.B.1.b].

The South Korean District Court had this to say about the manner in which the customary rule on State immunity should be interpreted. 'When interpreting and applying law [in this case the law on State immunity], *the results should be considered and if the interpretation leads to an unreasonable or unjust conclusion, measures should be taken to seek ways to exclude such interpretations.* To do so, several interpretative methods such *as logical and systematic interpretation*, historical interpretation, and *purposive interpretation* are utilized. … Interpreting that the Defendant is exempt from jurisdiction in a civil suit that was chosen as a forum of last resort in a case where the Defendant state destroyed universal values of the international community and inflicted severe damages upon victims *would result in unreasonable and unjust results*.[170] This is far from the only domestic court that has argued on the basis of logic and reasonableness. With respect to immunities for *jus cogens* violations the court in *A v Swiss Federal Public Prosecutor* was also of the view that '*it would be both contradictory and futile* if, on the one hand, we affirmed that we wanted to fight against these serious violations of the fundamental values of humanity, and, on the other hand, we allowed a broad interpretation of the rules of functional immunity'.[171] In *Her Majesty the Queen in Right of Canada v Edelson and others*, the court held that the purpose criterion, as distinct from that of legal nature, was not the appropriate one for distinguishing between *acta jure imperii* and *acta jure gestionis* because it would result in obliterating the distinction between private and State acts, and thus be absurd.[172] Finally, in the *Sea Shepherd* case the District court held that a broad interpretation of 'piracy' '[a]mong *other nonsensical results*, … would allow any seaman with a special affinity for a sea creature – say, a tuna – to state a piracy claim against a fisherman'.[173]

As far as *per analogiam* interpretations of CIL, the recent *Re Al M (Immunities)* in the UK High Court of Justice and the Court of Appeal is quite instructive. The applicant was the Head of Government of the United Arab Emirates. He commenced proceedings challenging the jurisdiction of the High Court and seeking the return of his two children. While the mother issued a number of applications, requesting *inter alia* that the children are made wards of court so that their removal is prevented. A number of judgements were delivered, but the one that is relevant here is the one considering the immunities of the

170 Ibid [3.C.3.6] (emphasis added).

171 *A v Swiss Federal Public Prosecutor* (n 167) [5.4.3] (emphasis added).

172 *Her Majesty the Queen in Right of Canada v Edelson and others* (n 156) [26] and [28]. A combined version of logical, teleological and systemic interpretation can also be seen in [22] and [26].

173 *Institute of Cetacean Research v Sea Shepherd Conservation Society*, 153 F.Supp.3d 1291 (WD Wash 2015) 1319.

Sheikh. Given that the immunities of Heads of Government are neither codified in any UK legal instrument or international treaty,[174] the High Court had to, as Webb puts it, 'wade into the murky waters of customary international law'.[175] The High Court rejected the comparison between the immunities of, on the one hand, diplomatic and consular agents, and on the other hand, the *troika*, ie Head of State, Head of Government and Minister of Foreign Affairs, because the scope of the respective immunities was different in at least one key aspect. The immunities of the former, save when in transit to or from a posting, apply only one foreign State – the receiving State.[176] Furthermore, in the High Court's view '[t]here can be no automatic assumption that a Head of Government is entitled in every foreign State to immunities of precisely the same scope as are accorded by the receiving State to the head of a diplomatic mission while posted in that State'.[177] Following on this, the High Court then examined whether an analogy could be made between the immunities accorded to Ministers of Foreign Affairs and those to Heads of Government. Referring to the *purposes* of such immunity (again an indication of teleological considerations being integral to the interpretation of CIL), it concluded that 'applying the same logic', while inviolability of Heads of Government may be required, the fact that inviolability is not the same as immunity from civil jurisdiction and that the immunity of a Head of Government is 'functional' 'then, provided he or she is personally inviolable while on official visits, we would incline to the view that the complete immunity from civil jurisdiction is not required to serve the purposes identified in the *Arrest Warrant* case'.[178] The Court of Appeal upheld the High Court's findings and noted that 'there is no exact equivalence between a Head of Government and Head of State, no matter how logical a development that might be'.[179]

Although the UK courts in the end rejected the expansive interpretation of the immunities of Heads of Government, and irrespective of whether one agrees with the conclusion of the UK courts to break apart the *troika* as a unit

---

174 Unlike the immunities of Heads of State which are regulated under Sections 1, 14 and 20 of the State Immunity Act (1978) <https://www.legislation.gov.uk/ukpga/1978/33> last accessed 1 October 2023.

175 P Webb, 'The Weakest Link of the Troika? The Immunity of Heads of Government in Customary International Law' (*EJILTalk!*, 27 October 2021) <https://www.ejiltalk.org/the-weakest-link-of-the-troika-the-immunity-of-heads-of-government-in-customary-international-law/> last accessed 1 October 2023.

176 *Re Al M (Immunities)* (19 March 2021) High Court of Justice [2021] EWHC 660 (Fam) [48].

177 Ibid [48].

178 Ibid [49–50]; citing also in support J Foakes, *The Position of Heads of State and Senior Officials in International Law* (OUP 2014) 125.

179 *Re Al M (Permission to Appeal)* (9 June 2021) Court of Appeal [2021] EWCA Civ 890 [23].

of analysis and to recognize different types of immunities as applicable to each of them,[180] the reasoning does seem to suggest that *per analogiam* constructions may have a role to play in the interpretation of customary international, but such interpretations must be approached with great care and scrutiny.

Although the examples discussed in this Section are far from exhaustive, they do demonstrate clearly not only that domestic courts are also active actors engaged in the interpretation of CIL, but also that there are certain interpretative methods that seem to be especially useful in the interpretation of CIL, thus, leading domestic courts to often rely on them.

5 Boundless or Bounded Interpretation?: the Conundrum of In/correct Interpretations

In the previous Sections it was demonstrated that CIL is not only interpretable but has also been the object of interpretation both in international and domestic jurisdictions. The inescapable question that logically follows from this, then, is how far can such an interpretation go? As has been seen multiple times before, such a question is not source-specific, ie it is not one that is tied to the function of CIL alone, but is rather one that is connected to the characteristics of legal interpretation as a process.

Hart's oft quoted passage that every legal rule has a 'core of settled meaning' but also a 'a penumbra of uncertainty'[181] is predicated on an understanding that there exist sets of correct and incorrect interpretations.[182] A core of settled meaning and a penumbra of uncertainty require the existence of a frame of reference outside these two, ie on the one hand one has the core of settled application and the penumbra of uncertainty, and then on the other hand there is something outside of these two. This would be the surrounding space where the rule's scope and interpretation cannot penetrate. This surrounding space would include among others, interpretations that clearly go beyond the limits of the legal rule's scope, ie incorrect interpretations.

A sub-set of such interpretations, known as perfidious interpretations, are nothing new under the sun. Authors of classical antiquity, such as Cicero, Polybius, Polyaenus, Thucydides, Valerius Maximus and Titus Livius[183] have in their

180 For some critical thoughts on this see Webb (n 175).

181 HLA Hart, 'Positivism and the Separation of Law and Morals' (195) 71/4 Harvard Law Review 607.

182 On the concept of 'correct interpretation' and its understanding as a 'set' see Merkouris (n 28).

183 Marcus Tullius Cicero, *De Officiis*, 1.40; Polybius, *Histories*, 3.27–3.29, 12.6; Polyaenus, *Stratagems*, 3.2; Thucydides, *The Peloponnesian War*, 3.34.3, 5.1.1–5.18.11, 6.2.1–6.2.6; Valerius

writings recorded several instances of such perfidious interpretations of ancient 'treaties'/agreements, where the extreme emphasis on the letter of the text to the detriment of the other interpretative elements, such as context, object and purpose, intention, led to interpretations done in bad faith. These have also been reproduced and further analysed in the context of international law by both Grotius and Vattel as a 'not to do' template in the case of interpretation of international agreements.[184]

This, of course, raises the question of whether in contemporary international law such an approach, embracing the existence of sets of correct and incorrect interpretations, has survived. In order to answer this, I shall now turn the focus of this study first to treaty interpretation, which has been the subject of closer scrutiny and debate and then extrapolate any conclusions arrived at to CIL. A good starting point is to examine the approach of the bodies, from where the rules that eventually became Articles 31–3 VCLT emerged and which are widely considered to reflect CIL. These rules emerged after lengthy discussions in three main *fora*, the *Institut de Droit International*, the ILC and the Vienna Conference on the Law of Treaties. It is to these discussions that this study will now turn to and examine whether any views were expressed as to whether 'in/correct interpretations' exist in international law.

In the 1956 Grenada Session, where the *Institut de Droit International* adopted its 'Resolution on Interpretation of Treaties' several members sided with the view of the existence of a correct interpretation. Fitzmaurice, in his role as *Rapporteur*, referred to de Visscher and expressed the view that 'the main purpose of interpretation was to find the true scope/meaning of the text to be interpreted',[185] while Accioly and de la Pradelle distinguished between the apparent, and ordinary meaning respectively and the 'true meaning' of the agreement of the parties.[186]

An argument often raised against the very existence of rules of interpretation, is that this was hotly contested even within the ILC as well as whether such rules should be even included in the draft articles on the law of treaties that the

---

Maximus, *Valeri Maximi Factorum et Dictorum Memorabilium*, 7.3.4; Titus Livius (Livy), *Ab Urbe Condita*, 21.18–21.19.

184 See H Grotius, *The Law of War and Peace* [*De Jure Belli ac Pacis*] (1625) Book II, Ch XVI 'On Interpretation'; E de Vattel, *The Law of Nations; or Principles on the Law of Nature: Applied to the Conduct and Affairs of Nations and Sovereigns* (1702), Book II, Ch XVII; see also, D Bederman, *Classical Canons: Rhetoric, Classicism and Treaty Interpretation* (Ashgate 2001).

185 Insitut de Droit International, 'IV. Délibérations de l' Institut en séances plénières: Quatriéme Question – De l' interprétation de traités' (1956) 46 AIDI 317, 321.

186 Ibid 328–9 and 330 respectively.

ILC was preparing.[187] Despite this the ILC not only eventually adopted rules of interpretation, but also explicated on this presumed inconsistency in their approach. In its view 'the Commission confined itself to trying to isolate and codify the comparatively few general principles which appear to constitute general rules for the interpretation of treaties. Admittedly, the task of formulating even these rules is not easy, but the Commission considered that *there were cogent reasons why it should be attempted. … In addition the establishment of some measure of agreement in regard to the basic rules of interpretation is important not only for the application but also for the drafting of treaties* (emphasis added)'.[188] In the end, the ILC opted for what is known as the 'crucible approach'.[189]

But what of the 'correct interpretation'? This was actually mentioned both by the USA and *Special Rapporteur* Waldock, when discussing whether recourse to supplementary means should be always permitted or only if the application of then draft Article 69 (now Article 31 VCLT) was 'not sufficient to *establish the correct interpretation* (emphasis added)'.[190] The *Special Rapporteur* went a step further, when discussing what became Article 31(3)(b), when he opined that '[c]learly, on the plane of interpretation, *the treaty has only one correct interpretation* (emphasis added)'.[191] The ICJ as well, has especially within the context of provisional measures, also utilised to the concept of 'correct interpretation'.[192]

The ILC, recently revisited issues of interpretation, when it examined the influence of subsequent agreements and practice in the interpretation of treaties. In 2018, the ILC adopted its 'Draft Conclusions' on this topic. Of import is Draft Conclusion 7 which provided that '[s]ubsequent agreements and subsequent practice under Article 31, paragraph 3, contribute, in their interaction with other means of interpretation, *to the clarification of the meaning of a treaty. This may result in narrowing, widening, or otherwise determining the range of possible interpretations, including any scope for the exercise of discretion*

187 See, for instance, the commentary to draft Article 27 (precursor of Article 31 VCLT); ILC 'Draft Articles on the Law of Treaties with Commentaries' (n 27) 218 [1–4].

188 Ibid 218–9 [5].

189 Ibid 220 [8].

190 ILC, 'Sixth Report on the Law of Treaties, by Sir Humphrey Waldock, Special Rapporteur' (11 March–14 June 1966) UN Doc A/CN.4/186 and Add.1–7 reproduced in [1966/II] YBILC 51, 93 and 99–100 [19–20].

191 Ibid 90 [9]. Earlier, in 1964, again when discussing subsequent practice, the ILC, referring to the writings of Fitzmaurice, had expressed a similar view; ILC, 'Third Report on the Law of Treaties by Sir Humphrey Waldock, Special Rapporteur' (3 March, 9 June, 12 June and 7 July 1964) UN Doc A/CN.4/167 and Add.1–3, reproduced in [1964/II] YBILC 5, 55.

192 Eg in *Application of the International Convention on the Elimination of All Forms of Racial Discrimination* (*Qatar v United Arab Emirates*) (Provisional Measures) [2018] ICJ Rep 406 [27].

which the treaty accords to the parties (emphasis added)'. This seems to give somewhat mixed signals. However, in the commentary the ILC clarifies that what it meant was not that there 'may ultimately be different interpretations of a treaty, but rather that the treaty may accord the parties the possibility to choose from a spectrum of different permitted acts'.[193] Just to make sure it made its point it also cited Lord Steyn in *House of Lords in R v Secretary of State for the Home Department, ex parte Adan* that 'there can only be one true interpretation of a treaty. ... In practice it is left to national courts, faced with a material disagreement on an issue of interpretation, to resolve it. But in doing so it must search, untrammelled by notions of its national legal culture, for the true autonomous international meaning of the treaty. And there can only be one true meaning'.[194]

6 Precautions/Limits of Interpretation

The existence of sets of correct and incorrect interpretations raises the question of whether there are any sign-posts or guidelines that delineate the point or area where one moves from the core of settled meaning (or even the penumbra of uncertainty) into clearly incorrect interpretation and may act as a 'North star' by which the interpreter can navigate the mercurial waters of interpretation and application. In this Section, this will be the focus of analysis, and Sections 7, 8 and 9 then will examine the potential transposability of any identified interpretative limits to the interpretation of CIL rules.

Although this is a somewhat under-researched area, even in the case of treaty interpretation, it is generally acknowledged that there are certain inherent limits to interpretation, or as Lord Sankey opined in *Edwards v. Attorney-General for Canada*,[195] although legal rules are 'living tree[s] capable of growth and expansion' nonetheless such growth and expansion should be 'within [the rule's] natural limits'.[196] Along the same vein, and in the context of international law, Judge Bedjaoui referred to such limits as 'precautions'.[197] These

193 ILC, 'Draft Conclusions on Subsequent Agreements and Subsequent Practice in Relation to the Interpretation of Treaties, with Commentaries' [2018/II – Part Two] YBILC 16, 53–4 [10] note 258.

194 Ibid 53–4 [10].

195 Albeit while interpreting a domestic instrument.

196 *Edwards v Attorney-General for Canada* (18 October 1929) Judicial Committee of the Imperial Privy Council [1930] AC 124, 136 per Lord Sankey.

197 *Gabčíkovo-Nagymaros Project (Hungary/Slovakia)* [1997] ICJ Rep 7, Separate Opinion of Judge Bedjaoui [5].

treaty interpretation limits/'precautions' are reflections of the restrictions imposed by the nature either of the system or of the rule itself. In the first category belong the limits of the principle of non-retroactivity and of *jus cogens*. What this means is that an interpretation cannot be such that it would either violate the principle of non-retroactivity[198] or conflict with a *jus cogens* rule.[199] Especially, with respect to the latter, this logically stems from the very definition of *jus cogens*, ie a rule from which no derogation is possible. Consequently, no interpretation, evolutive or other, is allowed to go against *jus cogens* rules.[200]

The *Institut* came to the same conclusion in its exploration of whether there are limits to the dynamic interpretation of the constitution and statutes of international organizations by their respective internal organs. Both in the 2021 Resolution and the 2019 Report the Institut's Seventh Commission emphasised 'that the dynamic interpretation by international organizations of their constituent instruments may not violate *jus cogens* [norms]'.[201]

In the instrument-oriented limits one can find the limit that interpretation should always observe the general rule laid down in Articles 31–3 VCLT or its customary counterpart[202] (and its various elements, eg text, context, and intention).[203] A violation of this limit may lead to a misinterpretation due to

---

198 ATA *Construction, Industrial and Trading Company v the Hashemite Kingdom of Jordan* (Award of 18 May 2010) ICSID Case No ARB/08/2 [109]; *Mondev International Ltd v* USA (n 124) [70].

199 *Application of the Genocide Convention* (n 123), Joint Declaration of Judges Shi and Koroma [2]; *South-West Africa (Second Phase) (Liberia and Ethiopia v South Africa)* [1966] ICJ Rep 6, Dissenting Opinion of Judge Tanaka 293–5; see also M Kotzur, 'Intertemporal Law' [2008] MPEPIL 1433 [13]; Th Georgopoulos, 'Le droit intertemporel et les dispositions conventionnelles évolutives: quelle thérapie contre la vieillesse des traités?' (2004) 108/1 RGDIP 123, 146.

200 ILC, 'Draft Conclusions on *Jus Cogens*' (n 47), Draft Conclusion 20 and accompanying Commentary.

201 Institut de Droit International, '7th Commission – Report: Are there Limits to the Dynamic Interpretation of the Constitution and Statutes of International Organizations by the Internal Organs of such Organizations (with Particular Reference to the UN System)? – Rapporteur M Arsanjani' (*IDI*, 2021) 30, Draft Resolution [5] <https://www.idi-iil.org/app/uploads/2021/05/Report-7th-commission-interpretation-statutes-international-organizations-vol-81-yearbook-online-session.pdf> last accessed 1 October 2023. The *Institut* also noted 'internationally protected fundamental human rights'. The disjunctive constructive of the sentence would imply that these would be fundamental human rights that have not achieved *jus cogens* status.

202 Unless, of course, the parties have agreed to different rules of interpretation, given the *jus dispositivum* nature of the rules of interpretation. In that case, the agreed upon interpretative rules form the new limit/'precaution'.

203 *Gabčíkovo-Nagymaros Project* (n 197) Separate Opinion of Judge Bedjaoui [5] and [7]; *Soering v* UK, EctHR, App No 14038/88 (7 July 1989) [103]; *Al-Saadoon and Mufdhi v* UK,

methodologically incorrect application of the interpretative rules[204] or in its extreme to a violation of another limit, namely that of interpretation amounting to a revision of the treaty.[205] Since it is only the parties to the treaty, or any appropriately so authorised body, that have that power, such an act amounts to judges exercising a *pouvoir de légiférer* that they have not been imbued with and cannot qualify as interpretation.[206]

This final limit of not conflating interpretation with amendment/modification is nothing new under the sun. Although interpretation is a distinct legal construct from amendment and modification, their boundaries have never been easy to discern and scholars have voiced their concerns over an oftentimes methodological *laissez faire* attitude of international courts and tribunals with respect to that distinction.[207]

EctHR, App No 61498/08 (2 March 2010) [119]; *Albert and Le Compte v Belgium*, EctHR, App No 7299/75 (10 February 1983) Partly Dissenting Opinion of Judge Matscher [3]; *Feldbrugge v Netherlands*, EctHR, App No 8562/79 (29 May 1986), Joint Dissenting Opinion of Judges Ryssdal, Bindschedler-Robert, Lagergren, Matscher, Sir Evans, Bernhardt and Gersing [24].

204 See for examples Section 9.

205 *Gabčíkovo-Nagymaros Project* (n 197) Separate Opinion of Judge Bedjaoui [5]; *Kasikili/Sedudu Island (Botswana/Namibia)* (Judgment) [1999] ICJ Rep 1045, Declaration of Judge Higgins [2]; *Case Concerning a Boundary Dispute between Argentina and Chile Concerning the Frontier Line between Boundary Post 62 and Mount Fitzroy (Argentina v Chile)* (1994) 22 UNRIAA 3 [157] (hereinafter *Laguna del Desierto*); *Claude Reyes and others v Chile* (Merits, Reparations and Costs) IACtHR Series C No 151 (19 September 2006) Separate Opinion of Judge Ramírez [1] and [3].

206 *Bayatyan v Armenia* [GC] EctHR, App No 23459/03 (7 July 2011) Dissenting Opinion of Judge Gyulumyan [2]; *Meftah and others v France* [GC] EctHR, App No 32911/96 (26 July 2002) Concurring Opinion of Judge Lorenzen joined by Hedigan; see also H Thirlway, 'The Law and Procedure of the International Court of Justice 1960–1989: Part One' (1989) 60 BYIL 1, 142; D French, 'Treaty Interpretation and the Incorporation of Extraneous Legal Rules' (2006) 55 ICLQ 281 296–7; ST Helmersen, 'Evolutive Treaty Interpretation: Legality, Semantics and Distinctions' (2013) 6 EurJLegStud 127, 137.

207 D Tladi, 'Is the International Law Commission Elevating Subsequent Agreements and Subsequent Practice?' (*EJILTalk!*, 30 August 2018) <https://www.ejiltalk.org/is-the-international-law-commission-elevating-subsequent-agreements-and-subsequent-practice/> last accessed 1 October 2023; the ILC also has recognised that especially in the case of bilateral treaties it may be difficult to distinguish whether subsequent practice amounts to modification (referring to the example of the *Air Transport Services Agreement* case [*Case Concerning the Air Service Agreement of 27 March* (USA *v France*) (1978) 18 UNRIAA 417]) or an authentic interpretation of the treaty (referring to the example of the *Temple of Preah Vihear* case [*Case Concerning the Temple of Preah Vihear* (*Cambodia v Thailand*) (Merits) [1962] ICJ Rep 6]); ILC, 'Report of the International Law Commission Covering the Work of its Sixteenth Session' (11 May–24 July 1964) UN Doc A/5809 reproduced in [1964/II] YBILC 173, 198 [2]; ILC 'Sixth Report' (n 190) 87–91 [1–15] and in particular [8]; ILC, 'Report of the International Law Commission on the Work of its Eighteenth Session' 4 May–19 July 1966) UN Doc A/6309/Rev.l, reproduced in [1966/II] YBILC 172, 236 [1].

The difficulty of drawing clear boundaries between interpretation and amendment/modification is also nothing surprisingly novel. During the ILC's work on the law of treaties, this was central to the whole discussion surrounding Draft Article 68.[208] Most parts of that Draft Article never went through to the Vienna Conference on the Law of Treaties, except for a sub-paragraph that dealt with modification by subsequent practice. The reason for the retention of this sub-paragraph was that although there was concern among the ILC members that 'the line may sometimes be blurred between interpretation and amendment of a treaty through subsequent practice'[209] they felt that these two processes were distinct and had to be treated as such, namely through the inclusion of a separate article.[210] However, in the Vienna Conference the concerns that such a provision may conflict with the principle of *pacta sunt servanda* and be open to abuse, led to its eventual deletion from the final text of the VCLT.[211]

Despite the sad history of the demise of Draft Article 68, the ILC members were of the view that interpretation and amendment were two distinct processes, and despite the inherent difficulties of such task, one should not bleed into the other. This was recently re-confirmed both by the ILC and the *Institut*. The ILC in its Draft Conclusion 7(3) on 'Subsequent Agreements and Subsequent Practice in Relation to Interpretation of Treaties', erred on the side of caution, opting for a presumption in favour of interpretation rather than amendment/modification, namely in the form that '[i]t is presumed that the parties to a treaty, by an agreement or a practice in the application of the treaty, intend to interpret the treaty, not to amend or to modify it.'[212] In the ILC's view,

208 Relating to the manner in which a treaty could be modified.

209 ILC 'Report on the ILC's Sixteenth Session' (n 207) 198 [2]; ILC, 'Summary Record of the 766th Meeting' (15 July 1964) UN Doc A/CN.4/SR.766 [122] (Waldock); ILC, 'Summary Record of the 767th Meeting' (16 July 1964) UN Doc A/CN.4/SR.767 [37] (Verdross), [39] (Waldock), [41] (Pal), [43] (Ago), [44–5] (Yasseen), [46–50] (Tunkin); ILC, 'Waldock Third Report' (n 191) [25].

210 ILC 'Report on the ILC's Sixteenth Session' (n 207) 198 [2]; ILC, 'Summary Record of the 866th Meeting' (9 June 1966) UN Doc A/CN.4/SR.866 [4] (Castrén), [7–8] (Jiménez de Aréchaga), [11] (Ago), [26] (Briggs), [36] (Yasseen). Against: ILC 'Summary Record of the 767th Meeting' (n 209) [35] (Verdross), [36] (de Luna); ILC 'Report on the ILC's Eighteenth Session' (n 207) 300 (Israel).

211 United Nations Conference on the Law of Treaties, '1st Session – 37th Meeting of the Committee of the Whole (COW)' (24 April 1968) UN Doc A/CONF.39/11 203 [60] (Venezuela), [61] Vietnam, [63] (France), [70] (Spain), [75] (Chile); United Nations Conference on the Law of Treaties, '1st Session – 38th Meeting of the Committee of the Whole (COW)' (25 April 1968) UN Doc A/CONF.39/11 210 [3] (Russia), [6] (USA), [30–2] (Guinea), [38] (Tanzania), [40] (Cuba), [42] (Portugal), [47] (Netherlands), [53] (Czechoslovakia).

212 ILC 'Draft Conclusions on Subsequent Agreements' (n 193) 58.

if the interpretative limits are crossed then we find ourselves in treaty modification territory, although it admitted that clear boundaries between the two processes may be difficult to draw and refused to take a clear position as as to whether modification of a treaty by subsequent practice of the parties was customary law.[213] The *Institut* for its part, citing Hexner, also shared the view that interpretation should not amount to amendment, although similarly to the ILC acknowledged that clearly outlining such boundaries would be a difficult task indeed.[214] Furthermore, in the same vein as the ILC it also went for an interpretative presumption in operative paragraph 7 of its Draft Resolution, where it suggests that 'unless otherwise provided in the constituent instrument of the international organization, when there is a general agreement among the membership of the international organization as to an interpretation, the interpretation should be presumed to be lawful and *intra vires*'.[215] Along the same line of thinking as the ILC, the *Institut* opted for a solution where the (rebuttable) presumption is that the subsequent agreement of the parties as to an interpretation, should be considered as exactly that an interpretation and not an amendment, the latter being of course *ultra vires*.

In sum, despite inherent difficulties interpretation and amendment/modification are treated as two separate processes. Interpretation may change the meaning of the treaty but amendment and modification may result in the changing of the text of the treaty.[216] Consequently, amendment/modification acts as a limit to the interpretative exercise. If that were not the case, judges would be granted a *pouvoir de légiférer*, which they have not. As Dupuy

213 Ibid 58–9.

214 The *Rapporteur* elaborated on this in the Report by referring again to Hexner, who touches upon the critical issue of interpreting the interpretive limits and also the amendment procedures: 'The question may be asked whether the interpretative power includes the right to determine the limits of the interpretative power, and whether it extends to interpretation of provision relative to amendments of the Agreement (Article XVII). The answer to this question is in the affirmative, subject, of course, to the fact that matters touching on *compétence de la compétence* frequently border on political aspects and involves problematical elements of *ultra vires* actions'; Institut de Droit International, '7th Commission – Report: Are there Limits to the Dynamic Interpretation of the Constitution and Statutes of International Organizations by the Internal Organs of such Organizations (with Particular Reference to the UN System)? – Rapporteur M Arsanjani' (2019) 78 AIDI 87, 198 citing P Hexner, 'Interpretation by Public International Organizations of their Basic Instruments' (1959) 53 AJIL 341, 350.

215 Institut de Droit International (n 201) 31, Draft Resolution [7].

216 C Djeffal, *Static and Evolutive Treaty Interpretation: A Functional Reconstruction* (CUP 2016) 15–6.

succinctly notes in this context, '[m]emory must remain loyal and not serve to rewrite history; a treaty belongs to its authors and not to the judge'.[217]

7 Jus Cogens Norms as a Limit in the Interpretation of Customary International Law

Let us then examine the transposability of the aforementioned limits/'precautions' to the interpretation of CIL. That an interpretation of a rule cannot be such that it would go against a rule of *jus cogens*, is a logical one and stems effortlessly from the definition of *jus cogens* rules, ie rules from rules from which no derogation is permissible and their consequent hierarchically superior normativity. The *Institut de Droit International* in its 1975 resolution on 'Intertemporal Law', considered it such a fundamental limit that 'States and other subjects of international law [although having] the power to determine by common consent the temporal sphere of application of norms ... [such power is] subject to any imperative norm of international law which might restrict [it]'.[218] Naturally, the ILC was examining cases of treaty interpretation but the rationale behind the *Institut's* relevant provision does not seem to be source-specific. The ILC has confirmed this, and overall the function of *jus cogens* rules as an interpretative limit for all rules irrespective of their source, in a number of reports produced in the context of several of its research topics. The ILC when working on 'Identification of Customary International Law' did not make any explicit statement on the interpretation of customary law, as this fell outside the scope of the ILC's topic, but it did highlight the fact that the Draft Conclusions were 'without prejudice to questions of hierarchy among rules of international law, including those concerning peremptory norms of general international law (*jus cogens*)'.[219]

If we turn our attention then to the more recent work of the ILC on '*Jus cogens*' we can see that Draft Conclusions 14 and 20 proposed by the Drafting Committee take a cradle to grave approach as to how *jus cogens* rules affects CIL in all the stages of its life-cycle, ie not only with respect to its emergence and termination (Draft Conclusion 14) but also its interpretation (Draft Conclusion 20). More specifically, Draft Conclusion 14, on the one hand, provides

217 P-M Dupuy, 'Evolutionary Interpretation of Treaties: Between Memory and Prophecy' in E Cannizzaro (ed), *The Law of Treaties Beyond the Vienna Convention* (OUP 2011) 123, 129.

218 Institut de Droit International, 'Resolution of 11 August 1975: The Intertemporal Problem in Public International Law' (1975) 56 AIDI 536 [3].

219 ILC 'Draft Conclusions on CIL Identification' (n 14), Commentary to Draft Conclusion 1 [5]; Draft Conclusion 15(3); Commentary to Draft Conclusion 15 [10].

that '1. [a] rule of customary international law does not come into existence if it conflicts with a peremptory norm of general international law (*jus cogens*) … 2. A rule of customary international law not of a peremptory character ceases to exist if and to the extent that it conflicts with a new peremptory norm of general international law (jus cogens)'.[220] Draft Conclusion 20, on the other hand, tackles the interpretation and application of rules in a manner consistent with peremptory norms of general international law, and provides that '[w]here it appears that there may be a conflict between a peremptory norm of general international law (*jus cogens*) and another rule of international law, the latter is, as far as possible, to be interpreted and applied so as to be consistent with the former'.[221] It is worth mentioning that Draft Conclusion 20 not only does not differentiate on the basis of source, but that this was an intentional choice as this Draft Conclusion was proposed by the Drafting Committee as an alternative to earlier versions of conclusions relating to the same matter that had somewhat different wording depending on the source.[222]

Jus cogens as a limit to the interpretative exercise is so pervasive and ubiquitous that it also comes up in other research topics of the ILC. Most notably, *Special Rapporteur* Concepción Escobar Hernández in her fifth report on 'Immunity of State Officials from Foreign Criminal Jurisdiction' and in the context of analysing possible limits and exceptions to the customary rule on immunities of State officials had the following to say regarding the interplay between customary law and *jus cogens*, making connections as well to the ILC's earlier work on 'State Responsibility'.

> In its reasoning, the Commission also includes another element of considerable interest in relation to the primacy of peremptory norms, noting that sometimes a conflict between primary norms need not be resolved by means of the secondary rules concerning responsibility. On the contrary, '[w]here there is an apparent conflict between primary obligations, one of which arises for a State directly under a peremptory norm of general international law, it is evident that such an obligation must prevail. *The processes of interpretation and application should resolve such questions*',

220 ILC, 'Peremptory Norms of General International Law (*jus cogens*): Text of the Draft Conclusions and Draft Annex Provisionally Adopted by the Drafting Committee on First Reading' (29 May 2019) UN Doc A/CN.4/L.936, Draft Conclusion 14 (1)–(2).

221 Ibid, Draft Conclusion 20 [10(3)] and [17(2)].

222 Cf ILC, 'Third Report on Peremptory Norms of General International Law (*jus cogens*) by Dire Tladi, Special Rapporteur' (12 February 2018) UN Doc A/CN.4/714, proposed Draft Conclusions 10, 15 and 17.

> given that '*peremptory norms of general international law generate strong interpretative principles which will resolve all or most apparent conflicts*'.[223]

The nature of *jus cogens* as rules from which no derogation is permissible has as a logical corollary that no interpretation of primary norms of a *non jus cogens* nature can arrive at such an interpretative outcome that it would lead to a conflict with a *jus cogens* rule. As an example of this, taken from a domestic legal system, the Central District Court of Seoul in the *'Comfort Women'* case, used *jus cogens* as a limit when interpreting the law of State immunity. In its judgment it held that given the consensus of the international community required for the emergence of a rule of *jus cogens* 'it can be said that a distinction exists between peremptory norm (*jus cogens*), which is a higher norm, and a lower norm. The lower norm should not deviate from *jus cogens*'.[224] The same logic was also followed in *A v Swiss Federal Public Prosecutor*.[225]

As both the ILC in the 2001 ARSIWA and *Special Rapporteur* Hernández in 2016 highlight, *jus cogens* norms 'generate strong interpretative principles' and '[t]his type of "conforming interpretation" could therefore be of particular importance … for the purpose of finding an appropriate balance among various primary norms'.[226] In this sense, *jus cogens* norms not only function as an interpretative limit that can resolve most apparent conflicts, but also and at the same time are part of the normative environment that shall be taken into account when interpreting customary rules, ie are 'relevant rules' in the version of 'systemic interpretation' analysed above in Sections 3–4.[227]

8 Revision as a Limit in the Interpretation of Customary International Law

Another limit that is applicable both to treaty interpretation and interpretation of CIL is that interpretation should never lead to an amendment/modification/revision of the rule in question. In the context of interpretation of CIL this has been a common recurring theme in a number of domestic cases. UK courts, for instance, have consistently, eg in the *Re Al M (Immunities)*, *Freedom*

---

223 ILC 'Fifth Report' (n 18) [136] citing also ARSIWA (n 101) 85, Commentary to Article 26 [3] (emphasis added).

224 *'Comfort Women'* case (n 160) [3.C.3.5].

225 *A v Swiss Federal Public Prosecutor* (n 167) [5.4.3].

226 ILC 'Fifth Report' (n 18) [136].

227 Which in the ILC's report is alluded to as 'conforming interpretation' as it ensures that customary rules conform with *jus cogens* norms.

and Justice Party and *Jones* cases, held that '[i]t is not for a national court to "develop" international law by unilaterally adopting a version of that law which, however desirable, forward-looking and reflective of values it may be, is simply not accepted by other states'.[228] This quote is both a reference to the fact that the existence and content of rules of international law should be determined on the basis of the system in which they have emerged,[229] and to revision being a limit to the judges' discretion, since 'developing' CIL unilaterally is nothing other than an attempt at unilateral revision of the rule that is not permitted under international law.

A similar thread seems to go through judge *ad hoc* Kreća's criticism of the methodology and conclusions arrived at by the ICTY in a number of cases, as he voiced it in *Croatia-Serbia Genocide* case. In his view, the manner in which the ICTY had interpreted CIL lacked rigor and consistency, and the content-determination of the customary rules in question resembled 'a quasi-customary law exercise based on deductive reasoning driven by meta-legal and extra-legal principles … [that] has resulted in judicial law-making through purposive [ie teleological], adventurous interpretation'.[230] The core of judge *ad hoc* Kreća's remarks is that, in his view, the ICTY by mis-applying the teleological approach to interpretation, ended up with a content of customary rules that went beyond their natural limits. In, essence, and this is clear from the use of the term 'judicial law-making', the judges had ended up revising/amending the customary rules in question, thus exercising a *pouvoir de légiférer* that they did not and should not possess, and had turned themselves from judges to legislators. Irrespective, of whether one agrees with this evaluation of the ICTY's pronouncements or not, the basis of judge *ad hoc* Kreća's opinion that in interpreting a CIL rule judges should not end up revising it is still valid.

The same debate about the line to be drawn between revision/modification of a customary rule is characteristic of the *Hadžihasanović* case. The rule in question was that of command responsibility, and the two main questions to be answered were, firstly whether command responsibility was applicable to

---

228 *Re Al M (Immunities)* (n 176) [15]; *R (Freedom and Justice Party) v Secretary of State for Foreign and Commonwealth Affairs* [2019] 2 WLR 578 [19] both citing *Jones v Ministry of the Interior of the Kingdom of Saudi Arabia (Secretary of State for Constitutional Affairs intervening)* [2007] 1 AC 270 [63] (Lord Hoffmann).

229 See in more detail below Section 9.2.

230 *Application of the Convention on the Prevention and Punishment of the Crime of Genocide (Croatia v Serbia)* (Merits) [2015] ICJ Rep 3, Separate Opinion of Judge *ad hoc* Kreća [91–2]; citing also in support M Swart, 'Judicial Law-Making at the *Ad Hoc* Tribunals: The Creative Use of Sources of International Law and "Adventurous Interpretation"' (2010) 70 Heidelberg Journal of International Law 459, 463–8, 475–8.

non-international armed conflicts as well, and second whether it survived a change in the persons in the chain of command, ie whether a superior was responsible for acts committed by his/her subordinates prior to the date s/he assumed command. While Judge Shahabuddeen was of the view that a teleological interpretation was appropriate,[231] the Tribunal was of the view that there did not exist sufficient practice and *opinio juris* to warrant such a conclusion and that, thus, extending the rule of command responsibility to cover situations such as those in *Hadžihasanović* would amount to extending the rule beyond its natural limits.[232]

What both *Croatia-Serbia Genocide* and *Hadžihasanović* highlight is the wider *problématique* of where the line is to be drawn between, on the one hand, interpretation and, on the other hand, revision/modification. This is, indeed, an extremely complex issue that lies at the very heart of content-determination. However, as has been shown multiple times already, this it is not a problem that is specific to CIL alone. Rather, it cuts through all sources of international law.

In the context of treaties, for instance, Gardiner addresses the critical issue of whether there is any practical importance attached to the exercise of distinguishing between interpretation and amendment/modification. Although, he recognises that in some scenarios there can be a blurring between the practical effects of the two, he very clearly lands on the side of the importance of distinguishing between the two. In his view, this is not like waiting for Godot.[233] Such an aphoristic equation between the two processes fails to take into account 'the importance of treaty relations, procedural difficulties, and [the effect of] decisions of courts and tribunals'.[234] The ILC confirmed this in its Draft Conclusion 7 on 'Possible effects of subsequent agreements and subsequent practice in interpretation' and the corresponding commentary. Although it admitted that a clear line may be difficult to draw, nonetheless such a distinction should not be overlooked nor cast aside as a mere technicality. As the ILC highlights 'States and international courts are generally prepared to accord parties a rather wide scope for the interpretation of a treaty by way of a subsequent agreement. … The recognition of this scope for the interpretation of a treaty goes hand in hand with the reluctance by States and courts to recognize that an agreement relating to the application of a treaty actually has the effect of

231 See in more detail above, Section 3.
232 In detail see Fortuna (n 73).
233 R Gardiner, *Treaty Interpretation* (2nd edn, OUP 2015) 275.
234 Ibid 275.

amending or modifying the treaty'.[235] It is this necessity of a distinction between the two processes that prompted the ILC not only to include Draft Conclusion 7 in its final outcome, but also to adopt, in paragraph 3 of that Conclusion, the rebuttable presumption that the parties to a treaty intend, through subsequent agreements or practice, 'to interpret the treaty, not to amend or to modify it'.[236]

What should one take away from this? First, that the distinction between interpretation and amendment/modification of a rule is not endemic to a particular source of international law, namely CIL but it permeates all sources, including treaties. Second, that amendment/modification has been recognised both in the case of treaties and of CIL as a limit to the interpretative exercise. Third, that the distinction has practical relevance. Interpretation, on the one hand, allows a rule to adapt but within the limits already provided by the rule. Amendment/modification, on the other hand, can go beyond that and against what was the intent of the parties (in the case of treaties) or what was allowed under the *ratio* of the existing State practice and *opinio juris* (in the case of CIL). Finally, that such a discussion is part of the process of clarifying the rules of interpretation and ensuring better reasoned and more clearly substantiated claims as to the content of rules, be they conventional or customary.

9 Misinterpretation: the Rules of Interpretation as a Limit in the Interpretation of Customary International Law

Irrespective of where one lands on the issue of correct interpretation, namely if there is one correct interpretation or a range of permissible interpretations, at the point where the interpreter exceeds the interpretative limits,[237] a misinterpretation has occurred. Does such a misinterpretation, though, require a 'cognisant mis-interpreter'? As Arajärvi notes that would be an emphatic no.

---

235 ILC 'Draft Conclusions on Subsequent Agreements' (n 193) Commentary to Draft Conclusion 7 [21].

236 Ibid, Draft Conclusion 7(3). On the importance of distinguishing between interpretation and amendment/modification see M Kohen, 'Keeping Subsequent Agreements and Practice in Their Right Limits' in G Nolte (ed), *Treaties and Subsequent Practice* (OUP 2013) 34, 42–3; S Murphy, 'The Relevance of Subsequent Agreement and Subsequent Practice in the Interpretation of Treaties' in G Nolte (ed), *Treaties and Subsequent Practice* (OUP 2013) 82, 89; R Moloo, 'When Actions Speak Louder Than Words: The Relevance of Subsequent Party Conduct to Treaty Interpretation' (2013) 31/1 BerkJIntlL 39, 78.

237 See above Section 6.

> 'Misinterpretation' by definition is not concerned with motivations, but it simply refers to 'the act of forming a wrong understanding of something that is said or done, or an example of a wrong understanding'. In any case, evidence of deliberate misinterpretation of CIL is rare and mostly misinterpreters have adopted a lazy methodology or ignored rules of interpretation in evaluating practice and/or *opinio juris*.[238]

This situation may further be exacerbated by the fact that as far as CIL is concerned the methods of its identification and content-determination have often been criticised as 'methodological mayhem'.[239] Despite this though, even though this dark forest of uncertainty one can on occasion clearly identify situations where a lack of methodological rigour has led to a misinterpretation. In fact, it is exactly this point which acts as the strongest plea for clarity in the content-determination of CIL through an exploration of the methods of its interpretation, and it is to such instances that we will now turn our attention.

In the analysis to follow, a set of cases where a misinterpretation of a customary rule has occurred will be examined. The cases selected are taken both from the international and domestic legal systems to demonstrate that the lack of interpretative methodological rigour with respect to CIL has a pervasive effect. It affects not only international courts and tribunals but also domestic courts, which increasingly participate as architects of the (in)consistency of the international legal order.[240]

9.1 *Misinterpretation in International Case-Law*

The first two cases with which this analysis will start are the *EC-Biotech* and *Vattenfall AB and Others v Germany* cases. These have as an added bonus that

---

238 N Arajärvi, 'Misinterpreting Customary International Law: Corrupt Pedigree or Self-fulfilling Prophecy?' in P Merkouris, J Kammerhoffer and N Arajärvi (eds), *The Theory, Practice and Interpretation of Customary International Law* (CUP 2022) 40, 48.

239 Talmon (n 23); S Talmon, 'Determining Customary International Law: The ICJ's Methodology and the Idyllic World of the ILC' (*EJILTalk!*, 3 December 2015) <https://www.ejiltalk.org/determining-customary-international-law-the-icjs-methodology-and-the-idyllic-world-of-the-ilc/#more-13882> last accessed 1 October 2023; generally, on issues arising from a lack of methodological rigour, see N Banteka, 'A Theory of Constructive Interpretation for Customary International Law Identification' (2018) 39/3 MichJIntlL 301; L Blutman, 'Conceptual Confusion and Methodological Deficiencies: Some Ways that Theories on Customary International Law Fail' (2014) 25(2) EJIL 529.

240 J d' Aspremont, 'The Systemic Integration of International Law by Domestic Courts: Domestic Judges as Architects of the Consistency of the International Legal Order' in OK Fauchauld and A Nollkaemper, *The Practice of International and National Courts and the (De-)fragmentation of International Law* (Hart Publishing 2012) 141; see also ILA (n 146).

what occurred was not only an interpretation of any simple customary rule, but a customary rule on interpretation, and more specifically, the customary law equivalent of Article 31(3)(c) VCLT also known as the principle of systemic integration.[241,242]

In *EC-Biotech* the issue was whether an alleged general EC moratorium on approvals of biotech products and related measures taken by the EC member States were in violation of the WTO agreements. One of the arguments raised by the EC was that the Convention on Biological Diversity (CBD)[243] and the Biosafety Protocol[244] were 'relevant rules' that had to be taken into account when interpreting the WTO Agreements and particularly the SPS Agreement.[245] The complainants (USA, Canada and Argentina) all raised the objection that only the EC was bound by the Biosafety Protocol and thus did not constitute a 'relevant rule',[246] while the USA was also not a party to the CBD.[247]

The Panel came to that conclusion but going down a somewhat different path. It is noteworthy as well that the *EC-Biotech* case is often used as an argument that the notion of 'parties' of the principle of systemic integration must be interpreted as 'all the parties to the treaty' and not as 'parties to the dispute' (or any other less stringent variation compared to 'parties to the treaty', eg 'any one of the parties to the dispute' or 'some of' or 'any one of the parties to the treaty'; the latter may be relevant in situations, such as Advisory Opinions, where there are no parties to a dispute). Bearing this in mind two objections need to be raised. One on context, and one on methodology. On first reading, the Panel seems to advocate in favour of a restrictive interpretation of the term

241 In more detail on this principle see, P Merkouris (n 21); P Merkouris, 'Principle of Systemic Integration' [2020] MPEiPro 2866; C McLachlan, 'The Principle of Systemic Integration and Article 31(3)(c) of the Vienna Convention' (2005) 54/2 ICLQ 279; VP Tzevelekos, 'The Use of Article 31(3) of the VCLT in the Case Law of the ECtHR: an Effective Anti-Fragmentation Tool or a Selective Loophole for the Reinforcement of Human Rights Teleology?' (2010) 31/3 MichJIntlL 621.

242 The *Delimitation of the Continental Shelf between Nicaragua and Colombia beyond 200 Nautical Miles* could also feature as an example of misinterpretation, due to misapplication of the rules of interpretation of CIL. This has been analysed in more detail above in Sections 2 and 3, and the reader is kindly directed to those Sections.

243 1992 Convention on Biological Diversity (adopted 5 June 1992, entered into force 29 December 1993) 1760 UNTS 79.

244 2000 Cartagena Protocol on Biosafety to the Convention on Biological Diversity (adopted 29 January 2000, entered into force 11 September 2003) 2226 UNTS 208.

245 1994 Agreement on the Application of Sanitary and Phytosanitary Measures (SPS Agreement) (adopted 15 April 1994, entered into force 1 January 1995) 1867 UNTS 493.

246 *EC-Biotech* (n 98) [7.56–7.63].

247 Ibid [7.74].

'parties'.[248] According to the Panel's interpretation 'the rules of international law to be taken into account … are those which are applicable in the relations between the WTO Members'.[249] However, if one reads a bit further the Panel carefully articulates that the present case is not one where the alleged relevant rules are applicable to the parties to the dispute, but not all WTO members (ie one version of the expansive interpretation). 'We need not, and do not, take a position on whether in such a situation [of rules applying to all parties to the dispute but not all WTO members] we would be entitled to take the relevant other rules of international law into account'.[250] Consequently, although the Panel seems to be inclined towards a restrictive interpretation, it does not unequivocally say that this is going to be the correct interpretation in all scenarios.

However, the more interesting point is a methodological one. The Panel's interpretation of the principle of systemic integration is *self-contradictory*. Firstly, it has to be noted that, according to the DSU the law that the DSBs apply when interpreting the WTO Agreements is not the VCLT as such, but rather the customary rules on interpretation, which are reflected in the VCLT.[251] This may seem somewhat like splitting hairs but is crucial for purposes not only of proper methodology but also applicable law. Consequently, what the Panel was doing in *EC-Biotech* was interpreting the customary rule on interpretation. In fact, on numerous points in its analysis the Panel explicitly talks about 'interpreting' and its 'interpretation' of Article 31(3)(c).[252] And how exactly one may wonder does the Panel arrive at this interpretation? It does so by often referring to various provisions of the VCLT.[253]

---

248 Here it has to be clarified that 'parties to the treaty' seems to be more expansive than 'parties to the dispute'. The characterisation of the interpretation of 'parties' as restrictive is done on the basis of the restrictive or expansive effect on the set of rules that can be taken into account under Article 31(3)(c) VCLT (and its customary law equivalent). Thus, the literally expansive interpretation of the term 'parties' (ie parties to the treaty) has a restrictive effect to the set of rules falling under Article 31(3)(c), and the reverse is true for 'parties to the dispute' (which is literally more restrictive, but has an expansive effect on Article 31(3)(c)). In academic scholarship this way of characterizing the interpretation of 'parties' as restrictive of expansive based on the effect that this has on the rule of interpretation may be somewhat counter-intuitive but it is the one that has prevailed, and is used here in that sense.

249 *EC-Biotech* (n 98) [7.68].

250 Ibid [7.72].

251 Article 3.2 DSU.

252 *EC-Biotech* (n 98) [7.68–7.72].

253 Ibid [7.68–7.74] and the corresponding footnotes. Indicatively, the Panel refers apart from the text of Article 31(3)(c) VCLT *eo ipso*, to the text of Articles 18, 31(2)(a) and (b), 31(3)(a), 66 and even the ILC commentary to the draft Vienna Convention to support its interpretation.

It is exactly this heuristic hermeneutic strategy that is extremely problematic from a methodological point of view. Courts and tribunals do have a tendency to pay lip service to the fact that the customary rules of interpretation are enshrined in the VCLT,[254] but if one considers the extensive debate on the very existence, let alone on the actual wording of Article 31–3 VCLT, to say that Articles 31–3 VCLT *verbatim* are, and more importantly have been, CIL in that exact form may be somewhat of an oversimplification.[255] In the *EC-Biotech* case this issue becomes even more pronounced because the Panel refers to the linguistic choices made in 31(2)(a)–(b) and 31(3)(a) VCLT to make a *contextual* argument. In paragraph 7.68 and the corresponding footnote 243, the Panel has the following to say: '[w]e find further support for this view in the provisions of Article 31(3)(b). Article 31(3)(b), *which is part of the immediate context of Article 31(3)(c)*, provides that a treaty interpreter must take into account "any subsequent practice in the application of the treaty which establishes the agreement of the parties regarding its interpretation". Like Article 31(3)(c), this provision makes reference to "the parties"'.[256] The Panel then leans on the Appellate Body's and the Panel's interpretation of the term 'parties' of Article 31(3)(b) VCLT in a previous case, the *EC–Chicken Cuts* case,[257] to make the logical leap that because Article 31(3)(b) VCLT is part of the *immediate context* of 31(3)(c) the term 'parties' should have the same meaning in both provisions.

It is one thing to say that the rules of interpretation are reflected in the VCLT, and a completely different thing to say that all the elements in Articles 31–3 VCLT even in their precise linguistic structure and placement with respect to one another are identical to the smallest detail. This fiction fails even more miserably if one also takes into account the reference to other provisions of the VCLT, as one would have then to concede that the VCLT in its entirety is reflective of CIL.

Methodologically, the more appropriate and precise way to approach this exercise[258] would have been to acknowledge that the customary rules on

254 See, for instance: *Maritime Delimitation in the Indian Ocean* (n 53) [63]; *Jadhav* (n 57) [71].

255 On the debate surrounding the VCLT rules on interpretation, see the commentaries to Articles 31–3 of the 1969 and the 1986 VCLT, in: O Dörr and K Schmalenbach (eds), *The Vienna Convention on the Law of Treaties: A Commentary* (2nd edn, Springer 2018); O Corten and P Klein (eds), *The Vienna Conventions on the Law of Treaties – A Commentary* (OUP 2011); and Villiger (n 40).

256 *EC–Biotech* (n 98) [7.68] note 243 (emphasis added).

257 *European Communities – Customs Classification of Frozen Boneless Chicken Cuts – Appellate Body Report* (27 September 2005) WT/DS269/AB/R and WT/DS286/AB/R [2005/XIX] DSR 9157 [272–3].

258 Which may also eventually lead to the desired convergence of content, but without falling into any methodological pitfalls.

interpretation are being interpreted by reference to the VCLT. The VCLT is, thus, used as an interpretative element to decipher the content of the customary rules on interpretation, and in fact it acts as a 'relevant rule'. Of course, that is perfectly fine, with the small exception of the conclusion at which the Panel arrives. The Panel concludes that the customary law equivalent of Article 31(3)(c) VCLT should be interpreted as meaning 'relevant rules of international law applicable in the relations between the parties to the treaty'. Bearing in mind that as was demonstrated above what the Panel is doing is interpreting the customary law equivalent of Article 31(3)(c), this in actuality, when interpreting customary rules, should be adjusted to 'relevant rules of international law applicable in the relations between the States bound by the customary rule'. However, the 'relevant rule' to which the Panel refers is a VCLT article. Most importantly, for the purposes of this analysis, neither every State in the world, nor all WTO members, and *not even all parties to the dispute* are parties to the VCLT, since the USA has not ratified it and the EU by definition, being an international organisation cannot be party to the VCLT.

What this boils down to is that although the Panel seems to be leaning in favour of a restrictive interpretation of the customary law equivalent of Article 31(3)(c), what it actually does is apply the principle of systemic integration to interpret a customary rule, by referring to a relevant rule that is applicable to *neither* of the two parties to a dispute. Essentially, while it seemingly rejects an expansive interpretation of the customary rule enshrined in Article 31(3)(c) VCLT, in order to arrive at that conclusion it has relied almost in its entirety on an interpretative method that is an even more expansive version (almost akin to *in pari materia* interpretation) of what it purports to reject.[259] It is this type of methodological inconsistency that advocates in favour of a clarification of the rules of interpretation of CIL and of greater methodological rigour in judgments.

To demonstrate that this is not merely an outlier let us examine the more recent *Vattenfall AB and Others v Germany* case. This dispute arose out of Germany's decision to phase out the use of nuclear energy. According to the applicants this decision was in violation of a number of obligations under the Energy Charter Treaty (ECT).[260] The European Commission was also involved, as it had decided to intervene as a non-disputing party, by virtue of Rule 37(2)

259 For a detailed deconstruction see P Merkouris, 'Interpreting the Customary Rules on Interpretation' (2017) 19 ICLR 126, 148–50.

260 1994 Energy Charter Treaty (adopted 17 December 1994, entered into force 16 April 1998) 2080 UNTS 100.

of the ICSID Rules of Procedure for Arbitration Proceedings.[261] The decision that is the object of our examination is the 'Decision on the *Achmea* Issue'. As the Tribunal noted, this decision arose from the jurisdictional objection made by Germany, to the effect that by virtue of the *Achmea* judgment, rendered by the Court of Justice of the European Union (CJEU),[262] the ICSID Tribunal did not have jurisdiction. The *Achmea* judgment concerned a Bilateral Investment Treaty (BIT) between the Netherlands and Slovakia.[263] The CJEU ruled that the arbitration clause contained in that BIT had an adverse effect on the autonomy of EU law, and was therefore incompatible with it.[264] Following the *Achmea* judgment, the European Commission argued that this precedent could be applied not only to bilateral treaties, but also to multilateral ones, and, thus, this barred the ICSID Tribunal from establishing jurisdiction in *Vattenfall*.[265]

The issue pertinent to our analysis is that the European Commission argued that EU law could be considered a 'relevant rule' for the purposes of interpreting the ECT. The Tribunal held that

> [t]he [European Commission's] approach is unacceptable as it would potentially allow for different interpretations of the same ECT treaty provision. The Tribunal considers that this would be an incoherent and anomalous result and inconsistent with the object and purpose of the ECT and with the rules of international law on treaty interpretation and application ... It cannot be the case that the same words in the same treaty provision have a different meaning depending on the independent legal obligations entered into by one State or another, and depending on the parties to a particular dispute. The need for coherence, and for a single unified interpretation of each treaty provision, is reflected in the priority given to

---

261 ICSID, 'ICSID Rules of Procedure for Arbitration Proceedings' (*ICSID*, April 2006) 99 <https://icsid.worldbank.org/sites/default/files/ICSID%20Convention%20English.pdf> last accessed 1 October 2023.

262 *Case C-284/16 – Slowakische Republik v Achmea BV* (6 March 2018) CJEU [GC] ECLI:EU:C:2018:158 (hereinafter *Achmea*).

263 1991 Agreement on Encouragement and Reciprocal Protection of Investments between the Kingdom of the Netherlands and the Czech and Slovak Federal Republic (adopted 29 April 1991, entered into force 1 October 1992) <https://jusmundi.com/en/document/treaty/en-agreement-on-encouragement-and-reciprocal-protection-of-investments-between-the-kingdom-of-the-netherlands-and-the-czech-and-slovak-federal-republic-netherlands-slovakia-bit-1991-monday-29th-april-1991> last accessed 1 October 2023.

264 *Achmea* (n 262) [57–62].

265 *Vattenfall AB and Others v Germany* (Decision on the *Achmea* Issue of 31 August 2018) ICSID Case No ARB/12/12 [1–2].

> the text of the treaty itself over other contextual elements under Article 31 VCLT.[266]

It then continued:

> While the [European Commission] refers to the use of Article 31(3)(c) VCLT as a 'systemic or harmonious interpretation', the Tribunal finds that the effects of such an interpretation in the manner proposed in the [European Commission's] submissions would not ensure 'systemic coherence', but rather its exact opposite. It would create one set of obligations applicable in at least some 'intra-EU' disputes and another set of different obligations applicable to other disputes. This would bring uncertainty and entail the fragmentation of the meaning and application of treaty provisions and of the obligations of ECT Parties, contrary to the plain and ordinary meaning of the ECT provisions themselves.[267]

There are many issues to untangle here. Firstly, what is the applicable law *vis-à-vis* interpretation? Is it CIL or is the VCLT? The answer may depend on one's interpretation of Article 4 VCLT, which provides for the non-retroactivity of the VCLT by providing that the Convention 'applies only to treaties which are concluded by States after the entry into force of the present Convention *with regard to such States*'.[268] Should these terms be interpreted as meaning that Article 4 should be construed as applying on a bilateral/izable basis or as a *si omnes* clause, in the sense that *all* States parties to a multilateral treaty need to be parties to the VVCLT in order for it to apply? Although, some of the Commentaries to the VCLT seem to lean in favour of the former,[269] contrary views, in favour of *si omnes* approach have also been supported by well renowned scholars.[270]

266 Ibid [155–6].

267 Ibid [158].

268 Emphasis added.

269 Mainly for reasons of increased effectiveness of the VCLT, see Fr Dopagne, 'Article 4 – Convention of 1969' in O Corten and P Klein (eds), *The Vienna Convention on the Law of Treaties: A Commentary* (OUP 2011) 79, 82 [10]; Villiger (n 40) 112–3 [7–8]. In support of the bilateral/izable approach see also PV McDade, 'The Effect of Article 4 of the Vienna Convention on the Law ofTreaties 1969' (1986) 35 ICLQ 409, 505; EW Vierdag, 'The Law Governing Treaty Relations Between Parties to the Vienna Convention on the Law of Treaties and States Not Party to the Convention' (1982) 76 AJIL 779, 785.

270 '[I]t will be a long time before anything like the majority of existing treaties in effective operation will be treaties concluded between States both or all of which are parties to the ... Convention'); H Thirlway, *International Customary Law and Codification: An Examination of the Continuing Role of Custom in the Present Period of International Law* (Sijthoff

In our case this discussion is important because in the *si omnes* scenario the fact that several parties to the Energy Charter Treaty are not parties to the VCLT (namely Afghanistan, France, the EU, Iceland, Romania and Turkey) would mean that the applicable law would be the customary rules on interpretation. Contrarily, in the case of the bilateral/izable construction, the VCLT would be applicable since Germany is a party.[271] Although as mentioned, the VCLT commentaries seem to lean in favour of the bilateral/izable construction of Article 4 VCLT, the Tribunal was somewhat sibyllic in its approach. When discussing this issue, and although later referring to the VCLT but mainly because the European Commission had also done so, it had this to say:

> In order to derive meaning from Article 26 ECT, like all treaties, it must be interpreted in accordance with international law. *These are the principles of international law relating to treaty interpretation*, application, and other aspects of treaties, which render the ECT workable. *They are reflected in the VCLT*, and provide the framework through which all treaties are interpreted and applied.[272]

They language used seems to strongly suggest that the Tribunal was applying CIL.[273] That would mean then that all the following references to the VCLT, are done under the same kind of interpretative lens as in the *EC–Biotech* case, ie that the VCLT is used as a 'relevant rule' for the purpose of interpreting the customary rules on interpretation. In any event, irrespective of whether the Tribunal was applying the VCLT or CIL, the following analysis remains pertinent as in both cases it would highlight some methodological issues with respect to the interpretation of the rule of interpretation irrespective of whether *qua* CIL or *qua* conventional rule.

1972) 108. O'Connell also siding with this view, makes an analogy with the similarly worded Article 2 of Hague Convention (IV) (1907 Hague Convention (IV) Hague Convention (IV) Respecting the Laws and Customs of War on Land with Annex of Regulations (adopted 18 October 1907, entered into force 26 January 1910) 36 Stat 2277). Article 2 of Hague Convention (IV) clearly and explicitly supports the *si omnes* construction: 'the provisions contained in the present Convention, do not apply except between Contracting Powers, *and then only if all the belligerents are parties to the Convention*'; DP O'Connell, *International Law, Vol I* (2nd edn, Stevens and Sons 1970) 205.

271 The EU would not form part of the equation since it was participating as an intervening but non-disputing party.

272 *Vattenfall AB and Others v Germany* (n 265) [125] (emphasis added).

273 Arguably also out of a degree of deference to the fact that EU was involved in the dispute and the issue arose with respect to EU law therefore any pronouncement could also potentially be used with respect to disputes with the EU.

But that is not all. Although, the Tribunal seems to imply that the principle of systemic integration and its term 'parties' should be understood as 'parties to the treaty', the way it attempts to substantiate that is problematic. The main crux of the Tribunal's argument is that an expansive interpretation of the principle of systemic integration would lead to incoherence, as the same provision would have a different meaning 'depending on the independent legal obligations entered into by one State or another, and depending on the parties to a particular dispute', whereas a single unified interpretation of each treaty provision can be secured only through a restrictive interpretation of the customary law equivalent of Article 31(3)(c).[274] This in and of itself is an attempt at a teleological and *effet utile* interpretation.[275]

However, this line of reasoning makes certain very questionable assumptions. Firstly, that an expansive interpretation of the customary rule enshrined in Article 31(3)(c) would lead to different interpretations of the same provision depending on the parties to the dispute. This assumes that the principle of systemic integration does not have any other safety valve, and that once the 'parties' requirement is met, the rule would be immediately taken into account. That is not the case. This is exactly, what the term 'relevant' is designed to do. To allocate the appropriate interpretative *gravitas* to a rule, by considering a number of factors that offer insight as to the true intention of the parties. Not every rule would be automatically considered as 'relevant'. In fact, 'actor proximity' together with other forms of proximity,[276] would be taken into account to determine relevance. In the *Vattenfall* case, in fact, if the Tribunal had focused more on 'relevance' it would have arrived at the same conclusion, without committing methodological errors.

---

274 *Vattenfall AB and Others v Germany* (n 265) [156].

275 An argument could also be raised here as to whether the single unified interpretation, although a desirable result, and one that is quite compelling, is indeed a *sine qua non* of the interpretation of a treaty provision. For instance, in other parts of the VCLT the unified meaning and regulatory regime has been sacrificed in the altar of either ensuring greater participation (as in the case of reservations under Articles 19–22 VCLT) or greater applicability of the VCLT itself (see above the discussion on Article 4 VCLT).

276 On the 'proximity criterion' and the various manifestations of 'proximity' within Article 31(3)(c) both as treaty and as customary rule, see Merkouris 'Article 31(3)(c) and the Principle of Systemic Integration' (n 21) Ch 1; Merkouris 'Principle of Systemic Integration' (n 241) [34–7].

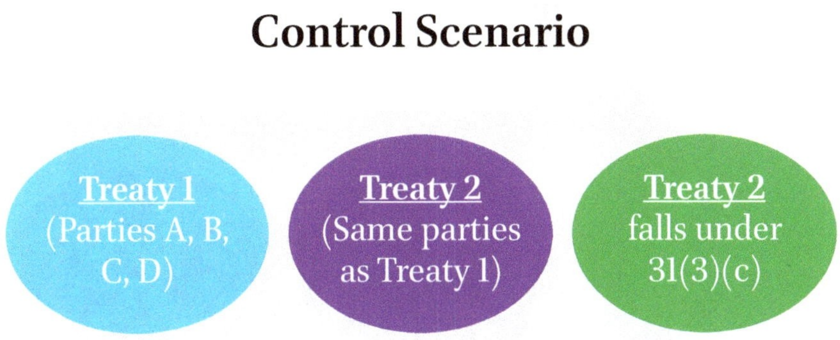

FIGURE 2 Control scenario of 'Stability' of 'Parties to the Treaty'

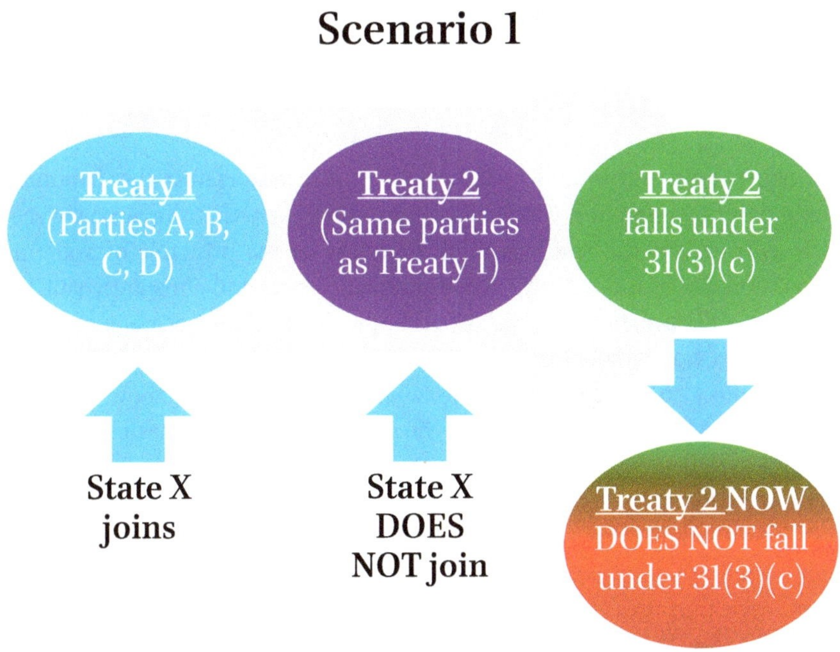

FIGURE 3 Scenario 1 of 'Stability' of 'Parties to the Treaty'

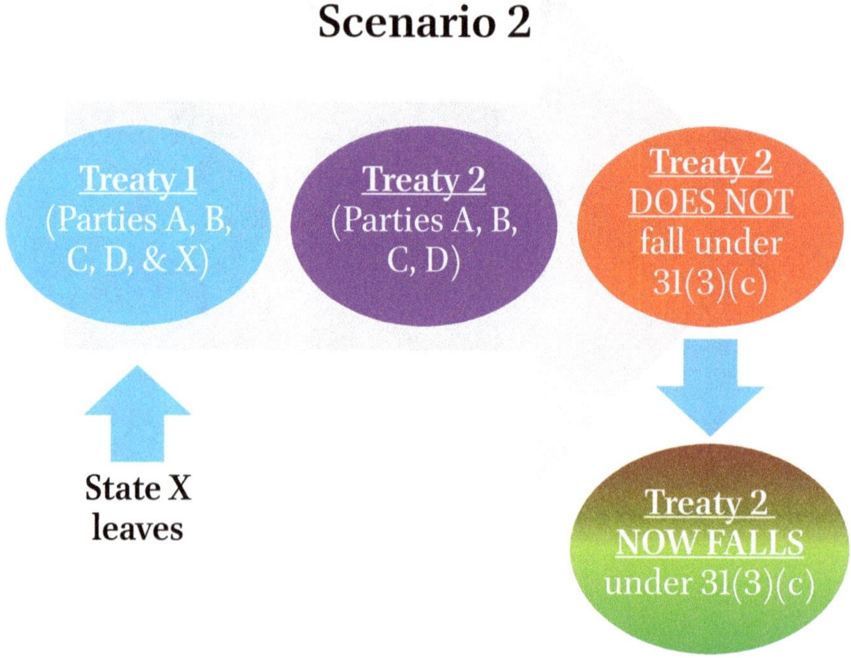

FIGURE 4 Scenario 2 of 'Stability' of 'Parties to the Treaty'

Furthermore, and to add to the criticism directed against the Tribunal's claim about incoherence, it actually seems more likely that the opposite scenario is true. It is the restrictive interpretation of the principle of systemic integration that is more likely to lead to incoherence, and constantly shifting meanings of provisions. The reason is simple. Every time a State acceded to or withdrew from the treaty being interpreted, the set of potential 'relevant rules' would also change (see Figures 2–4; in all the figures below the term 'same parties' has been used to make the example clearer and easier to follow. Treaty 2, may have additional parties, not parties to Treaty 1).

To make matters even worse, this would also be true for any accession or withdrawal to any other treaty of any of the State parties, as this would also affect whether that treaty and its articles could be considered 'relevant' for interpretative purposes (see Figures 5 and 6).

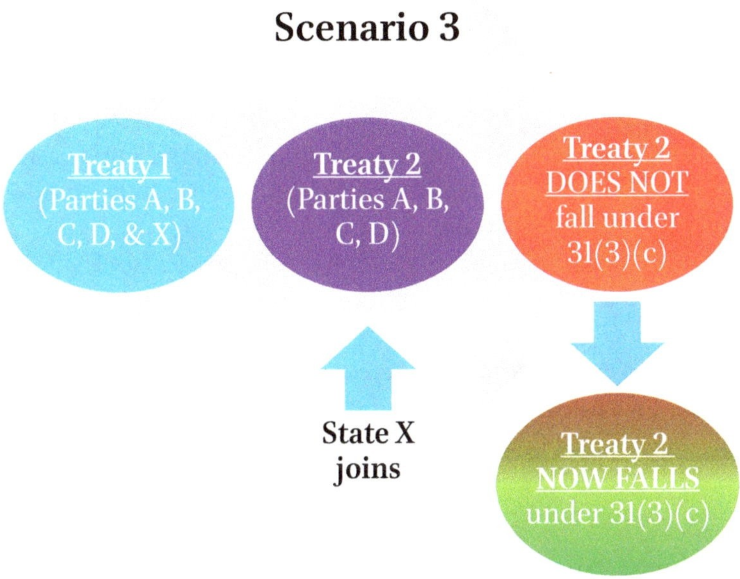

FIGURE 5 Scenario 3 of 'Stability' of 'Parties to the Treaty'

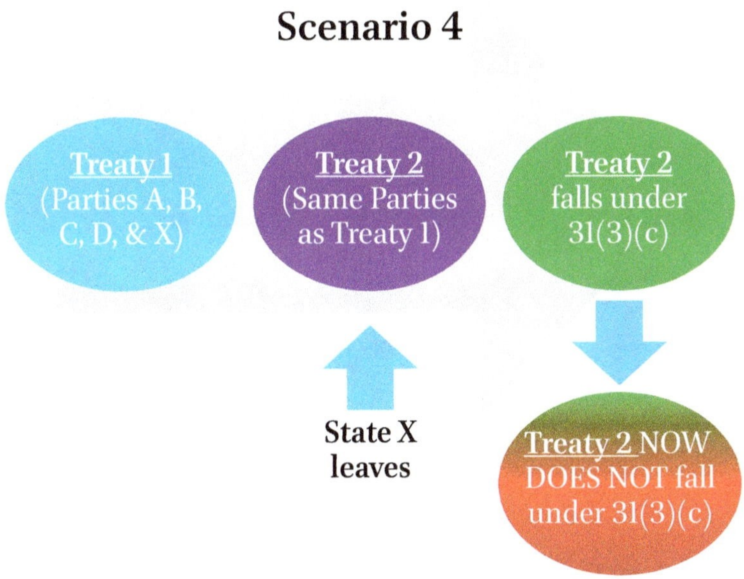

FIGURE 6 Scenario 4 of 'Stability' of 'Parties to the Treaty'

On the other hand, an expansive reading of the principle of systemic integration, ie as referring to 'parties to the dispute' (or any other less stringent variation compared to 'parties to the treaty') where the focus is more on determining actual 'relevance' may increase the pool of potential 'relevant rules', but ensures greater stability and coherence as the 'actor proximity' is not the only decisive criterion, but needs to be supplemented by other forms of proximity, to a degree that would satisfy the interpreter.

The above are presented schematically in the following images (see Figures 7 and 8):

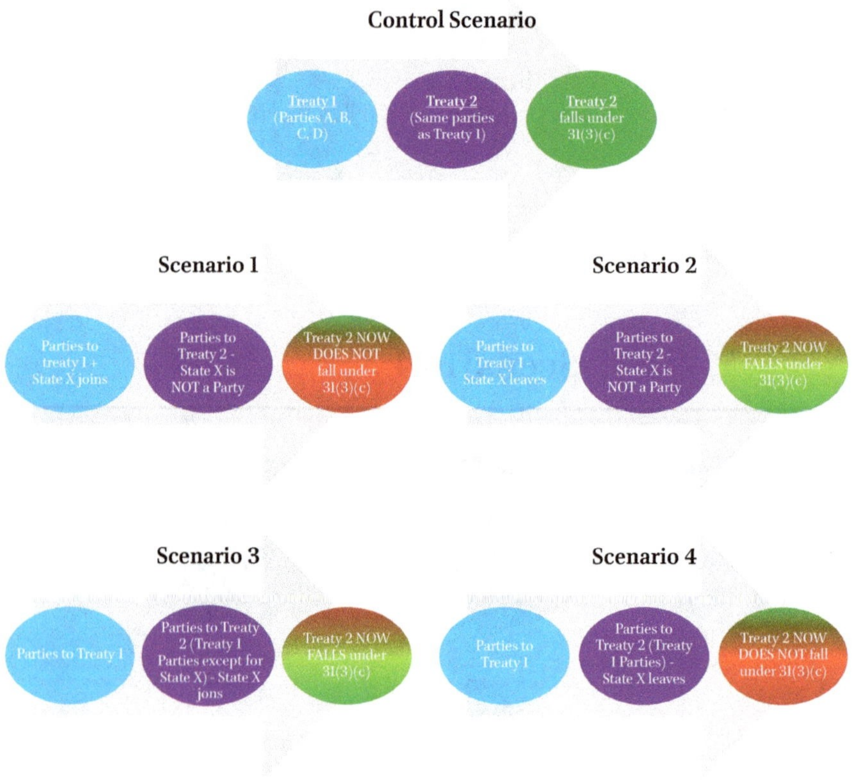

FIGURE 7 Consolidated scenarios of 'Stability' of 'Parties to the Treaty'

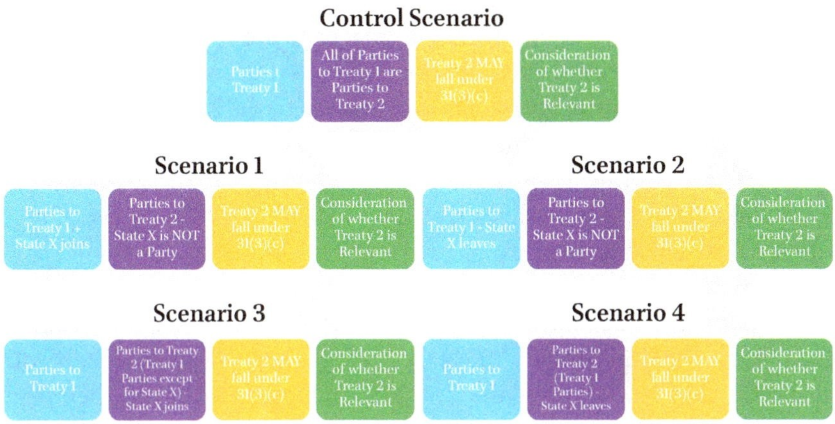

FIGURE 8 Consolidated scenarios of stability of 'Parties to the Dispute' and/or other less strict interpretations of 'Parties'

Thus, somewhat paradoxically, it is the expansive interpretation that better ensures the systemic coherence that the Tribunal in *Vattenfall* so fervently argued for.[277] This misapplication of the *telos* of the customary rule known as the 'principle of systemic integration', should not detract from the fact that although done erroneously what the Tribunal attempted was a teleological interpretation. What is unfortunate is that had the Tribunal properly applied the customary law equivalent of Article 31(3)(c) VCLT it would have arrived at the same result, as will be explained immediately below, without the need for resorting to a misinterpretation of the customary rule.

To further our criticism of the *Vattenfall* Tribunal's reasoning one need not go further than a few paragraphs following the discussion on what 'parties' meant. The Tribunal referred to a number of other reasons that buttressed its finding,

277 This line of reasoning is also supported by the jurisprudence of other courts and tribunals, such as the European Court of Human Rights (ECtHR), (eg in *Demir and Baykara v Turkey* [GC] ECtHR, App No 34503/97 (12 November 2008) [67]; *National Union of Rail, Maritime and Transport Workers* (*RMT*) *v* UK, ECtHR, App No 31045/10 (8 April 2014) [76]; *Graziani-Weiss v Austria*, ECtHR, App No 31950/06 (18 October 2011) [36]; *Pini and Others v Romania*, ECtHR, App Nos 78028/01 and 78030/01 (22 June 2004) [139–42]) and the Inter-American Court of Human Rights (IACtHR) (eg in *Ituango Massacres v Colombia* (Preliminary Objections, Merits, Reparations and Costs) IACtHR Series C No 148 (1 July 2006) [157]; *The Right to Information on Consular Assistance in the Framework of the Guarantees of the Due Process of Law* (Advisory Opinion) IACtHR Series A No 16 (1 October 1999) [112–5]). In more detail, see Merkouris 'Principle of Systemic Integration' (n 241) [25–37].

such as that there are inherent limits to the interpretative discretion of a judge, in the sense that any use of 'relevant rules' should not lead to an interpretation that would conflict with the text and the object and purpose of the ECT,[278] the lack of subject-matter and linguistic proximity between the ECT and the Dutch-Slovak BIT to which the *Achmea* judgment invoked by the EU referred.[279] However, the most important seems to be the discussion on the fact that no 'rule' had actually been invoked, as the EU had simply referred to EU law as a whole rather than specifying a particular rule that would trigger the application of Article 31(3)(c).[280]

From both a judicial economy and methodological perspective this seems akin to putting the cartwheel before the horse. Any examination of whether the rule enshrined in Article 31(3)(c) VCLT comes into play should start with an examination of whether a 'rule' first and foremost exists. If not, then there was really no point in discussing either 'parties' or 'relevant'. It is, thus, not surprising that post-*Vattenfall* awards have been more careful, and rightly so, in focusing on the 'non-revision/non-re-writing' limit of Article 31(3)(c), the 'rules' aspect and the 'relevant' aspect.[281] If one were to venture a guess, it seems likely that this example of misinterpretation by the *Vattenfall* Tribunal was the result of on the one hand, of the Tribunal objecting to the interpretation proposed by the EU, rather than to the relevance *eo ipso* of EU law,[282] and on the other hand, a more strategic/political choice to protect the investment dispute settlement system from EU's effort to give primacy to the EU judicial system.

9.2 *Misinterpretation in Domestic Case-Law*

Examples of misinterpretation are not, however, the prerogative solely of international courts and tribunals. In this Section, a few examples taken from domestic courts will be examined, where the interpretation of CIL, at least from an international law methodological perspective, seems to have gone somewhat beyond what the rules of interpretation prescribe.

278 *Vattenfall AB and Others v Germany* (n 265) [155–8].

279 Ibid [162].

280 Ibid [159–61].

281 See, for example *AS PNB Banka and others v Latvia* (Decision on the intra-EU objection of 14 May 2021) ICSID Case No ARB/17/47 [562–71]; *Silver Ridge Power BV v Italy* (Award of 26 February 2021) ICSID Case No ARB/15/37 [220–3]; *BayWa re renewable energy GmbH and BayWa re Asset Holding GmbH v Spain* (Award of 25 January 2021) ICSID Case No ARB/15/16 [229]; *Strabag SE and others v Poland* (Partial Award on Jurisdiction of 4 March 2020) ICSID Case No ADHOC/15/1 [8.125].

282 This is supported by *Vattenfall AB and Others v Germany* (n 265) [165].

The first case to consider is the *'Comfort Women'* judgment, delivered by the Central District Court of Seoul. The main issue of the judgment issued in 2021, was whether State immunity, which had been invoked by Japan, applied even in situations where grave crimes against humanity had been perpetrated.[283] In Section 4 the study examined the parts of the judgment where the Central District Court acknowledged the evolutive nature of the doctrine of State immunity[284] and engaged among others in a logical and teleological interpretation of it. However, in addition to this it based its reasoning on a 'systemic'/'harmonising' type of interpretation. The problem is that this 'systemic interpretation' was focused on domestic law rather than the system in which the rule had emerged, ie international law.

More specifically, the Central District Court noted that when interpreting the law, which includes in our case the customary law on State immunity, the interpretation should not lead to 'an unreasonable or unjust conclusion'. In order to avoid such interpretations, 'methods such as logical and systematic interpretation, historical interpretation, and purposive interpretation are utilized'.[285] So far so good, although it has to be noted that the Court is a bit unclear as to whether these methods are used as understood under international law or domestic law.[286] Similarly in a number of places the Court also referred to the fact that '[i]nterpreting that the Defendant is exempt from jurisdiction in a civil suit that was chosen as a forum of last resort in a case where the Defendant state destroyed universal values of the international community and inflicted severe damages upon victims would result in unreasonable and unjust results'.[287]

What creates a bit of an issue is what comes after that where the Court ties this need for reasonableness and harmonisation with the Constitution. This happens first when it links the interpretative methods to the Constitution,[288] but more clearly in the paragraph immediately after when it holds that

283 In detail see E Branca, '"Yet, it moves …": The Dynamic Evolution of State immunity in the "Comfort Women" case' (*EJILTalk!*, 7 April 2021) <https://www.ejiltalk.org/yet-it-moves-the-dynamic-evolution-of-state-immunity-in-the-comfort-women-case/?utm_source=mailpoet&utm_medium=email&utm_campaign=ejil-talk-newsletter-post-title_2> last accessed 1 October 2023.

284 And also implicitly recognised its potential for evolutive interpretation.

285 *'Comfort Women'* case (n 160) [3.c.3.6].

286 Although an argument could be made that there is significant overlap.

287 *'Comfort Women'* case (n 160) [3.c.3.6].

288 'These interpretation methods are constitutionally conforming interpretations that conform to the principles of the Constitution and the law and realize them as much as possible'; although it is still unclear again whether these are seen merely as domestic rules of interpretation, or as international ones that are in conformity with the Constitution; ibid [3.c.3.6].

an interpretation allowing Japan to invoke immunity in this case would deprive 'victims of their right of access to courts guaranteed by the Constitution and not providing a remedy for their rights. *Such results are unreasonable and unjust as they are not in accordance with the overall legal order that positions the Constitution as the highest norm*'.[289]

In sum, the Central District Court of Seoul focused on the fact that an expansive interpretation of State immunity would lead to a non-prosecution of crimes against humanity and that such a result would be unreasonable as it would conflict with the right of access to courts guaranteed by the Constitution. Because of this and in order to promote the harmonisation of the rules of Korean domestic legal system the Court opted for the restrictive interpretation of State immunity. As mentioned above the reasoning of the Court is a mélange of interpretation of CIL in its proper sense, ie using the interpretative tools of the international legal order, and an 'systemic integration' type of interpretation, where the system to which reference is made is not the international one but the domestic one. and in particular its own Constitution. What implications this has from a methodological point of view is something that will be discussed again at the end of this Section, but before doing that it would be beneficial to examine another case where a similar approach seems to have been followed.

In *Her Majesty the Queen in Right of Canada v Edelson and others* the Supreme Court of Israel engaged in a lengthy analysis of whether the signing of the contract (lease agreement) should be considered as an *actum jure imperiis* or an *actum jure gestionis*. When discussing the criteria to be applied in distinguishing between *acta jure imperii* and *acta jure gestionis* it also referred to its own domestic legal order, in a manner both similar and dissimilar as the previous case of the *Comfort Women*. Similar in the sense that it also connected the interpretative exercise to the domestic legal order, yet dissimilar in the sense that the emphasis was less on harmonisation and more on gap-filling. Although in earlier paragraphs, the Supreme Court of Israel engaged in a teleological interpretation of the CIL rule,[290] it attempted to reinforce its argument by alluding to the *lacunae* of the international customary rule.

> [P]ending the development of a standard international practice regarding this issue, it is inevitable that *each State will apply its own locally accepted criteria in accordance with its existing national jurisprudence* ... It is incumbent upon us to formulate a distinction that accounts for basic

289 Ibid [3.C.3.6.i] (emphasis added).

290 See also Section 4.

> values such as individual rights, equality before the law and the rule of law. This having been said, we will allow the foreign State to realize its sovereign objectives, without subjecting them to judicial review in a foreign state's courts. The balance struck between these conflicting considerations is far from simple and is certainly not immutable. *It would seem that, for the time being, it is sufficient to determine that, when in doubt, we must rule in favor of recognizing internal jurisdiction.* In any case, the tendency should be towards restricting immunity. This is our practice regarding any domestic matter.[291]

It is useful to note that in all the cases referred here, domestic courts have engaged in one way or another with international law, and CIL in particular. In this context then it is worth remembering the typology that the ILA Study Group on Principles on the Engagement of Domestic Courts with International Law identified. According to the ILA Study Group

> [w]hatever the contents of any norm of international law may be, there are broadly three ideal types of strategy or posture of domestic court engagement with international law, qualified by the outcome of such engagement. These are: the *posture* or *strategy of avoidance* (where the question of international law is altogether dodged); the *posture* or *strategy of alignment* (where – irrespective of the prescription of the constitutional framework, or even on the basis of an interpretation of such prescription which, on its face, seems to point towards avoidance – an attempt is made to align with international law or at least to harmonize domestic law or practice with international regulation); and the *posture* or *strategy of contestation* (where domestic law is ostensibly used as a method to contest the generally accepted content of existing international law ...).[292]

These strategies/postures can be further subdivided in: i) evasive or affirmative (for avoidance) ii) fair weather, overriding, consubstantial, hyper (for alignment); and iii) affirmative, negatory and consubstantial (for contestation).[293]

So what posture did the domestic courts adopt in the above-analysed cases, for what reason and what conclusions can one arrive at or what lessons can be

291 *Her Majesty the Queen in Right of Canada v Edelson and others* (n 156) [29–30] (emphasis added).

292 ILA (n 146) [37].

293 Ibid [39–42], [43–56] and [57–65] respectively.

learned? The answer is not that simple, because all the types of strategy/posture have the 'to collapse into another or to alternate depending on context and perhaps also on the particular reader's viewpoint'.[294] In *Comfort Women* and *Canada v Edelson and others* the domestic courts depending on one's view of the content of the CIL rule may have either adopted the posture/strategy of alignment or contestation. In *Comfort Women*, for instance, the domestic court attempted to align the content of the customary rule with the normative environment of the domestic legal system. In legal systems, an attempt at harmonising rules which emerge from different legal orders is often referred to as 'consistent interpretation'.[295] Although this principle has a bevy of manifestations depending on the domestic legal system, with, for instance, some applying it only for certain rules (eg only treaties) while others for all international rules regardless of their source, and with some requiring a level of ambiguity while others none.[296]

Although 'consistent interpretation' can fall under several of the types and sub-types of strategy/posture, ranging from alignment to contestation, the *Comfort Women* case presents us with a crucially different scenario. Whereas 'consistent interpretation' flows into one direction, with domestic law being interpreted in a manner that ensures consistency of the domestic law with international law, in *Comfort Women* the interpretative exercise seems to be flowing in the opposite direction, ie it is the CIL that is being interpreted in a fashion to ensure that it conforms or is harmonised with the domestic regulations, be they the Constitution or other instruments of a lower order. Essentially, this would be a 'reverse consistent interpretation'[297] or as Judge Nussberger characterised it in *Al-Dulimi v Switzerland* 'fake harmonious interpretation'.[298] Whether this example falls under alignment (of the consubstantial or hyper-alignment type) or under contestation of the affirmative type will depend on whether one considers that the arrived at conclusion as being in conflict or not with the content of the rule of CIL.

---

294 Ibid [50].

295 This has usually developed from the practice of the highest courts within the domestic legal system of States; this is the case for instance in the USA (the *Charming Betsy* principle being a prime example); Germany (where consistent interpretation is considered as flowing from the *Völkerrechtsfreundlichkeit* of the Basic Law); Austria (where it is known as 'Schubert-Praxis'); Italy; Switzerland; Australia; Canada; and South Africa. In more detail see ibid [51] note 51 and relevant State reports.

296 For examples see ibid [24] and the various State reports.

297 Ibid [58]; Ryngaert (n 73).

298 *Al-Dulimi and Montana Management Inc v Switzerland* [GC] ECtHR, App No 5809/08 (21 June 2016) Dissenting Opinion of Judge Nußberger.

Similar considerations also apply to *Canada v Edleson and others*, although there the issue was not primarily one of harmonisation, but rather of gap-filling. This situation would seem to be a more pronounced version of 'reverse consistent interpretation' and, if one takes an approach similar to the majority in *Hadzihasanovic* and *Oric*,[299] more leaning towards affirmative contestation.[300] If, however, one considers that the outcome was indeed the correct one, we are again in the realm of alignment. Irrespective of its classification there is a methodological problem with respect to 'fake harmonious'/'reverse consistent' interpretation at least from international law's frame of reference.

The existence and content-determination of CIL has to occur on the basis of the rules set by the system from which it emerged.[301] In a string of UK cases regarding immunity this has been one of the main points. To clarify, rules of CIL '[w]here they are not incompatible with statute, ... shape the common law unless there is some constitutional or other special reason why they should not'.[302] To identify the existence of a rule of CIL, the stringent standards set by international law (existence of practice and *opinio juris*) need to be met.[303] 'What is immediately apparent ... is that the ascertainment of customary international law involves an exhaustive and careful scrutiny of a wide range of evidence. Moreover, a finding that there is a rule of customary international law may have wide implications, including ... for the common law. ... "It is not for a national court to 'develop' international law by unilaterally adopting a version of that law which, however desirable, forward-looking and reflective

---

299 Where the lack of sufficient practice and *opinio juris* on the precise issue was *eo ipso* enough to declare that no such customary rule existed.

300 Affirmative contestation is defined as '[consisting] primarily in the domestic court accepting the validity or applicability of the international law norm but giving it a meaning different from that which is generally accepted, indicating thus that it wishes to change the content of the norm or that it perceives it as different from what is generally accepted'; ILA (n 146) [58].

301 See cases and analysis below; see also Ammann, who argues that '[d]omestic courts must take the characteristics of international lawmaking into account. Otherwise, they are not interpreting the *interpretandum*'; O Ammann, *Domestic Courts and the Interpretation of International Law* (Brill/Martinus Nijhoff 2020) 35; similarly, Ryngaert (n 73).

302 *Re Al M (Immunities)* (n 176) [12]; *R (Freedom and Justice Party) v Secretary of State for Foreign and Commonwealth Affairs* (n 228) [16] (Arden LJ); *Mighell v Sultan of Johore* [1894] 1 QB 149, 159–60 (Lord Esher MR); *Aziz v Aziz* [2008] 2 All ER 501 [55–61]; *Harb v Asic* [2014] 1 WLR 4437 [14] (Rose J) and [2016] Ch 308, [35–9] (Aikens LJ); *R v Bow Street Metropolitan Stipendiary Magistrate ex parte Pinochet Ugarte (No 3)* [2000] 1 AC 147, 201G–202A (Lord Browne-Wilkinson).

303 *Re Al M (Immunities)* (n 176) [14]; *Benkharbouche v Embassy of the Republic of Sudan* [2019] AC 777 [31]; *R (Freedom and Justice Party) v Secretary of State for Foreign and Commonwealth Affairs* (n 228) [16].

of values it may be, is simply not accepted by other states"'.[304] This particular quote highlights two issues. First, that the identification and content-determination of a rule of CIL must conform to the rules of the legal sphere from which it emerged, and second and closely connected to the first, that any such interpretation should not lead to a unilateral revision of the rule, which in and of itself would also be a violation of the rules of international law.[305] The point on conformity has also been explicitly acknowledged by the Italian Constitutional Court, which has held that '[i]nternational custom is external to the Italian legal order, and its application by the government and/or the judge … must respect the principle of conformity, ie must follow the interpretation given in its original legal order, that is the international legal order'.[306]

Ammann has suggested that these issues of problematic engagement with CIL by domestic courts may be due to the fact that as far as those courts are concerned the '"divide" between domestic and international law is anything but sharp … especially due to the proliferation of "inward-looking" international legal norms governing States' conduct within their own jurisdiction'.[307] It is not surprising that in the cases examined the common theme was that of State immunity.

An additional factor, complicating things, is the multifariousness of where States are situated in the spectrum of monism and dualism as well. International legal scholarship has introduced a number of terms to describe the set of possible overlaps between domestic and international norms, such as 'multi-sourced equivalent norms', 'consubstantial norms', and 'interface norms'.[308] The common nucleus of these terms is that they refer to 'norms which happen

304 *Re Al M (Immunities)* (n 176) [15]; *R (Freedom and Justice Party) v Secretary of State for Foreign and Commonwealth Affairs* (n 228) [19] both citing *Jones v Ministry of the Interior of the Kingdom of Saudi Arabia (Secretary of State for Constitutional Affairs intervening)* [2007] 1 AC 270 [63] (Lord Hoffmann).

305 On revision as a limit to the interpretative exercise, see in more detail Section 8.

306 *Sentenza No 238/2014* (22 October 2014) Italian Constitutional Court [3.1] (unofficial English translation available at <https://www.cortecostituzionale.it/documenti/download/doc/recent_judgments/S238_2013_en.pdf> accessed 1 November 2021).

307 Ammann (n 301) 34; see also JE Nijman and A Nollkaemper, 'Introduction' in JE Nijman and A Nollkaemper (eds), *New Perspectives on the Divide Between National and International Law* (OUP 2007) 1; CJ Tams and A Tzanakopoulos, 'Introduction: Domestic Courts as Agents of Development of International Law' (2013) 26 LJIL 531, 534.

308 See, respectively: T Broude and Y Shany (eds), *Multi-Sourced Equivalent Norms in International Law* (Hart Publishing 2011); ILA (n 146) [30]; N Krisch, 'Pluralism' in J d'Aspremont and S Singh (eds), *Concepts for International Law: Contributions to Disciplinary Thought* (Edward Elgar 2019) 691.

to exist both at the international and at the domestic level, and provide for the same substantive regulation (ie, they have the same substance)'.[309]

This lack of a clear divide is further exacerbated according to Ammann by clusters of difficulties. Among these she identifies the 'alleged lack of expertise and methodological rigor',[310] which would include the 'disregard or misapplication of the interpretative methods of international law' by national courts.[311] Other difficulties would include parochialism (ie, a neglect of the peculiarities of international law or even an avoidance of international legal issues),[312] judicial imperialism *vis-à-vis* other States, and the influence of domestic legal constraints[313] However, as this study has demonstrated, in the situations under examination the main issue would be one of methodological rigor, from an international law perspective, rather than let us say parochialism, as the domestic courts truly and genuinely engaged with the international legal system, in one way or another.

Two points need to be raised in this regard. Firstly, that although the methodological rigour criticism is somewhat applicable in the present case, as far as 'fake harmonious interpretation' is concerned, the domestic courts did in other parts of the judgment engage in interpretation of CIL proper,[314] as shown above in Section 4. Second, that although the methodological rigour may be somewhat spotty this is far from a trait of domestic courts alone. As the analysis in

309 ILA (n 146) [30]; A Tzanakopoulos, 'Domestic Courts in International Law: The International Judicial Function of National Courts' (2011) 34 LoyLAInt'l&CompLRev 133, 142–4.

310 Ammann (n 301) 41; see also A Nollkaemper, 'Decisions of National Courts as Sources of International Law: An Analysis of the Practice of the ICTY' in G Boas and WA Schabas (eds), *International Criminal Developments in the Case Law of the ICTY* (Brill/Martinus Nijhoff 2003) 277, 292.

311 Ammann (n 301) 322. Additional clusters of difficulty that Ammann identifies include: the lack of substantiation of the courts' interpretative assertions; the self-referentiality and even circularity of the case law; and the 'the imprecise terminology and uneven level of detail of domestic courts' reasoning on international law'; Ammann (n 301) 322. It has to be noted, however, that these difficulties are far from characteristic of domestic courts alone as has been shown in previous Sections.

312 On parochialism see E Benvenisti, 'Reclaiming Democracy: The Strategic Uses of Foreign and International Law by National Courts' (2008) 102 AJIL 241, 243–5; *contra* Y Shany, 'National Courts as International Actors: Jurisdictional Implications' (2009) 15 Rivista di diritto pubblico italiano, comunitario e comparato 1 <https://www.federalismi.it/ApplOpenFilePDF.cfm?artid=13810&dpath=document&dfile=29072009111203.pdf&content=National%2Bcourts%2Bas%2Binternational%2Bactors%3A%2Bjurisdictional%2Bimplications%2B%2D%2Bdottrina%2B%2D%2Bdottrina%2B%2D%2B> last accessed 1 October 2023.

313 Ammann (n 301) 41–2.

314 Although, again, in *Comfort Women* the reference was to interpretative principles recognised by the Constitution, which somewhat muddles the methodological waters.

Sections 3 and 9.1 has demonstrated international courts are equally open to that criticism. The reason is quite simple. The theoretical discussion of interpretation of CIL is still in a state of infancy, as, for instance, was the methodology surrounding treaty interpretation prior to the adoption of the common lexicon of the various draft codes on the law of treaties, and more importantly the VCLT. This underlines the purpose of the present contribution, namely that the interpretation of CIL is not only happening but demands our attention in order to promote greater clarity and methodological rigor in the content-determination of the rules stemming from this source.

10 Conclusion

Diogenes, the famous cynic famously harassed Plato on his definition of what a human is. The definition that had been proposed was 'an upright, biped being without feathers'. Not one to let a trolling opportunity be wasted, Diogenes showed up in Plato's Academy, and threw in the middle a plucked chicken and announced 'Behold, Plato's [hu]man'! Although Plato's amended definition post this encounter still left a lot to be desired,[315] and although clearly this was an interpretation done in bad faith, what one can take from this is that everything is open to interpretation, and that interpretation is ubiquitous. After all, who among us will not side with McDougal's famous takedown of the Vattelian axiom *in claris non fit interpretatio* as an 'obscurantist tautology'? Clarity can be achieved only through the process of interpretation.

But as far as international law is concerned, is this essential content-determinative function restricted only to written instruments? The answer is an emphatic no. Not only are there other examples of unwritten binding rules that are generally accepted to be interpretable, but also arguments that CIL cannot be interpreted because 'content merges with existence', fold upon closer inspection. This is because they are never premised solely on an evaluation of State practice, but in the interpretation of a rule that is either accepted as existing, or at least exists as a virtual/mental substitute in the mind of the judge in order for her/him to engage in methods that are classically interpretative in nature. For those, who insist on the need for some form of textuality, Alland's analysis of CIL being imbued with a form of 'lexical garment' seems to be the final *coup de grâce*.

International and domestic case-law as well seem to confirm this conclusion, with several instances of CIL interpretation in diverse specialised regimes

315 He simply added 'with broad flat nails'.

and areas of international law. *Telos*, 'by proxy' textual interpretation, systemic integration, evolutive interpretation, *effet utile*, *per analogiam* interpretation to name but a few, are tools in the interpretative arsenal that we are all familiar with, and they appear time and time again in CIL interpretation. What is the nature of these identified patterns or methods is a topic that falls outside the scope of the present study. But if I were to venture a mercurial guess, to also tip my hat to the Greek/Roman god whose name is etymologically associated with hermeneutics, I would say that this would be up for debate. If the examples provided, and the ones that exist in international and domestic practice, satisfy the threshold set by the two-element approach, they could be qualified as customary rules. However, one needs to remember that even with the treaty interpretation rules, whether these were indeed rules or something else was something that was hotly contested,[316] and even today still debated in some circles. But even if they are not considered CIL rules, then could they not be principles stemming from domestic legal systems? Again, here the question would be whether they satisfy the commonality to various legal systems and transposability requirements that the ILC in its recent work on the topic seems to suggest are the way to identify the existence of a general principle.[317] Irrespective of where one lands on this debate, there is also another option, either separate or supplementary to the ones already mentioned. The methods identified, the language used to describe them and the manner in which they are utilised is very reminiscent of the early attempts at codification of the law of treaties and of adopting a shared vocabulary on the interpretative process.[318] Given the rather limited academic engagement with CIL interpretation, it would seem that history repeats itself. The more we discuss and analyse these methods both in and of their own, and in comparison to other existing rules of interpretation, the more refined and increasingly more precise their content and application will become.

The nature of these methods notwithstanding, as with treaty interpretation so CIL interpretation is not unlimited. *Jus cogens*, revision and misapplication of the rules of interpretation outline these outer borders of CIL interpretation. These limits may not always be easily discernible, and there can be areas of uncertainty, but they are there, nonetheless, a judicial *sorites* waiting to be characterised as such.

316 The ILC when preparing the draft VCLT articles was very honest about this; ILC 'Draft Articles on the Law of Treaties with Commentaries' (n 27) 218 [1–4].

317 ILC, 'General Principles of Law: Texts and Titles of Draft Conclusions 1, 2 and 4 Provisionally Adopted by the Drafting Committee' (28 July 2021) UN Doc A/CN.4/L.955, Draft Conclusion 4.

318 See Section 3 and discussion on Fiore's draft code.

To conclude, the rumours of the impending death of CIL are rather unwarranted. Not only CIL remains one of the pillars of the international legal system,[319] but it is interpretable and its interpretation imbues it with the vivaciousness and negentropic qualities necessary for any rule (written or unwritten) to adapt and respond to circumstances that change at an increasing rate.

319 On par with the other two formal sources. Although see Prost, who argues that there are hierarchies between them but 'these hierarchies are not rigid, pre-determined, or definitive but rather fluid and transient'; M Prost, 'Sources and the Hierarchy of International Law: Source Preferences and Scales of Values' in S Besson and J d'Aspremont (eds), *The Oxford Handbook of the Sources of International Law* (OUP 2021) 640.

Annex: 2023 TRICI-Law Draft Guiding Principles on the Interpretation of Rules of Customary International Law

Panos Merkouris, Sotirios-Ioannis Lekkas, Marina Fortuna and Nina Mileva[320]

Guiding Principle 1: Scope

The present Guiding Principles concern the manner in which rules of customary international law are to be interpreted.

Guiding Principle 2: Interpretability of Rules of Customary International Law

Rules of customary international law are subject to interpretation.

Guiding Principle 3: Identification and Interpretation of Rules of Customary International Law

1. The identification of a rule of customary international law is a legal process distinct from the interpretation of that rule.
2. Identification focuses on determining the existence of a rule of customary international law on the basis of relevant general practice and its acceptance as law (*opinio juris*). Interpretation focuses on determining the content of the rule. Each of these processes is governed by different rules.

---

320 These draft Guiding Principles are based on research conducted in the context of the project 'The Rules of Interpretation of Customary International Law' ('TRICI-Law'). This project has received funding from the European Research Council (ERC) under the European Union's Horizon 2020 Research and Innovation Programme (Grant Agreement No. 759728).

The TRICI-Law team would like to thank all the contributors and participants to the various conferences and workshops organises and co-organised by TRICI-Law for their contributions and ideas. The TRICI-Law team would also like to express its gratitude especially to all the contributors of the last TRICI-Law, AthensPIL and UoA Conference, who discussed and provided feedback for the improvement of these draft Guiding Principles, Prof. Fay Pazartzis, Prof. Linos-Alexander Sicilianos, Prof. Hélène Ruiz Fabri, Mrs. Maria Telalian, Prof. Malgosia Fitzmaurice, Dr. Andre de Hoogh, Prof. Frans Nelissen, Dr. Efthymios Papastavridis, Prof. Vaios Koutroulis, Dr. Stravros Pantazopoulos, Prof. Marcel Brus, Prof. Patrícia Galvão Teles, Dr. Georgios Kyriakopoulos, Prof. Jan Wouters, Dr. Andreas Kulick, Dr. Jenny Stavridi, Prof. Concepción Escobar Hernández, Prof. Maria Gavouneli, Prof. Alessandra Gianelli, Dr. Eleni Micha and Dr. Anastasios Gourgourinis. Special thanks also go out to Mr. Emmanuel Giakoumakis, Mr. Nikiforos Panagis, Dr. Nikolaos Voulgaris, Mr. Ivo-Tarik de Vries-Zou, Mr. Konrad Turnbull, Dr. Jörg Kammerhofer, Dr. Noora Arajärvi, Dr. Riccardo di Marco, Prof. Pauline Westerman and Prof. Alette Smeulers, for their comments on and suggestions for these draft Guiding Principles. Naturally, all the views expressed here are the authors' alone.

Guiding Principle 4: Interpretation as a Single Combined Operation

1. A rule of customary international law, as previously identified, shall be interpreted in good faith in accordance with its object and purpose, its normative context and in a manner that does not deprive it of its effectiveness, as set out in the present Guiding Principles.
2. The interpretation of a rule of customary international law is a single combined operation, which places appropriate emphasis on the various means of interpretation indicated in the present Guiding Principles.

Guiding Principle 5: Teleological Interpretation

1. A rule of customary international law shall be interpreted with reference to its object and purpose.
2. The interpretation of a rule of customary international law may also take into account the object and purpose of the branch of law to which the rule of customary international law belongs.

Guiding Principle 6: Principle of Systemic Integration

The interpretation of a rule of customary international law shall take into account any relevant rules of international law.

Guiding Principle 7: Principle of Effectiveness

A rule of customary international law shall be interpreted in such a manner that does not deprive it of its effectiveness.

Guiding Principle 8: Evolutive Interpretation

A rule of customary international law may, where appropriate, be interpreted evolutively.

Guiding Principle 9: 'By Proxy' Textual Interpretation

1. Textual interpretation, in the strict sense, is not applicable to the interpretation of rules of customary international law.
2. In the interpretation of a rule of customary international law recourse may be had to a form of 'by proxy' textual interpretation, that is relying on the terms of a written text including, *inter alia*, provisions in treaties or other codifying instruments reflecting rules of customary international law.

Guiding Principle 10: Limits to Interpretation

1. There are limits to the interpretation of rules of customary international law.

2. Such limits include:
   a) An interpretation of a rule of customary international law may not, as far as possible, lead to an outcome that conflicts with a *jus cogens* rule.
   b) An interpretation of a rule of customary international law may not lead to an outcome that modifies the rule being interpreted.
   c) An interpretation of a rule of customary international law may not go beyond the principles of interpretation, as set out in these Guiding Principles.
3. Guiding Principle 10 is without prejudice to the development of additional limits.

Guiding Principle 11: Lex specialis

These Guiding Principles shall be without prejudice to the interpretation of rules of customary international law that is governed by special rules of international law.

Bibliography

Books & Chapters in Edited Volumes

Advisory Committee of Jurists, *Procès Verbaux of the Meetings of the Advisory Committee of Jurists: 16 June–24 July 1920 with Annexes* (van Langenhuysen 1920).

Allot Ph, 'Interpretation – an Exact Art' in A Bianchi, D Peat and M Windsor (eds), *Interpretation in International Law* (OUP 2015) 373.

Ammann O, *Domestic Courts and the Interpretation of International Law* (Brill/Martinus Nijhoff 2020).

Apalagaki Ch, *Code of Civil Procedure: Article by Article Interpretation, Articles 1–590* (4th edn, Nomiki Vivliothiki 2016).

Arajärvi N, 'Misinterpreting Customary International Law: Corrupt Pedigree or Self-fulfilling Prophecy?' in P Merkouris, J Kammerhoffer and N Arajärvi (eds), *The Theory, Practice and Interpretation of Customary International Law* (CUP 2022) 40.

Bederman D, *Classical Canons: Rhetoric, Classicism and Treaty Interpretation* (Ashgate 2001).

Bos M, *A Methodology of International Law* (Elsevier Science Publisher BV 1984).

Braumann C and A Reinisch, '*Effet Utile*' in J Klingler, Y Parkhomenko and C Salonidis (eds), *Between the Lines of the Vienna Convention? Canons and Other Principles of Interpretation in Public International Law* (Wolters Kluwer 2018) 47.

Broude T and Y Shany (eds), *Multi-Sourced Equivalent Norms in International Law* (Hart Publishing 2011).

Brownlie I, 'Some Problems in the Evaluation of the Practice of States as an Element of Custom' in G Arangio-Ruiz (ed), *Studi di diritto internazionale in onore di Gaetano Arangio-Ruiz, Vol I* (Editoriale Scientifica 2004) 313.

Byers M, *Custom, Power and the Power of Rules: International Rules and Customary International Law* (CUP 1999).

Corten O and P Klein (eds), *The Vienna Conventions on the Law of Treaties – A Commentary* (OUP 2011).

d' Aspremont J, 'Custom-making Moment in Customary International Law' in P Merkouris, J Kammerhofer and N Arajärvi, *The Theory, Practice and Interpretation of Customary International Law* (CUP 2022) 29.

d' Aspremont J, 'The Multidimensional Process of Interpretation: Content-Determination and Law-Ascertainment Distinguished' in A Bianchi, D Peat and M Windsor (eds), *Interpretation in International Law* (CUP 2015) 112.

d' Aspremont J, 'The Systemic Integration of International Law by Domestic Courts: Domestic Judges as Architects of the Consistency of the International Legal Order' in OK Fauchauld and J d' Aspremont, *The Discourse on Customary International Law* (OUP 2021).

de Vattel E, *The Law of Nations; or Principles on the Law of Nature: Applied to the Conduct and Affairs of Nations and Sovereigns* (1702).

Degan VD, *L'interprétation des accords en droit international* (Nijhoff 1963).

di Marco R, 'Customary International Law: Identification versus Interpretation' in in P Merkouris, J Kammerhoffer and N Arajärvi (eds), *The Theory, Practice and Interpretation of Customary International Law* (CUP 2022) 414.

di Marco R, *L'interpretazione del diritto consuetudinario* (PhD Thesis, Università di Roma Tor Vergata / Université Paris Nanterre, November 2022).

Djeffal C, *Static and Evolutive Treaty Interpretation: A Functional Reconstruction* (CUP 2016).

Dopagne Fr, 'Article 4 – Convention of 1969' in O Corten and P Klein (eds), *The Vienna Convention on the Law of Treaties: A Commentary* (OUP 2011) 79.

Dörr O and K Schmalenbach (eds), *The Vienna Convention on the Law of Treaties: A Commentary* (2nd edn, Springer 2018).

Droubi S and J d'Aspremont (eds), *International Organisations, Non-state Actors, and the Formation of Customary International Law* (MUP 2020).

Dupuy P-M, 'Evolutionary Interpretation of Treaties: Between Memory and Prophecy' in E Cannizzaro (ed), *The Law of Treaties Beyond the Vienna Convention* (OUP 2011) 123.

Elias O and CL Lim, *The Paradox of Consensualism in International Law* (Kluwer Law International 1998).

Fitzmaurice M and P Merkouris, *Treaties in Motion: The Evolution of Treaties from Formation to Termination* (CUP 2020).

Foakes J, *The Position of Heads of State and Senior Officials in International Law* (OUP 2014).

Fortuna M, 'Different Strings of the Same Harp: Interpretation of Customary International Rules, their Identification and Treaty Interpretation' in P Merkouris, J Kammerhofer and N Arajärvi (eds), *The Theory, Practice and Interpretation of Customary International Law* (CUP 2022) 393.

Fortuna M, *Interpretation of Customary International law in International Courts* (University of Groningen, 2023).

Gardiner R, *Treaty Interpretation* (2nd edn, OUP 2015).

Gautier P, 'Article 2 – Convention of 1969' in O Corten and P Klein (eds), *The Vienna Convention on the Law of Treaties: A Commentary* (OUP 2011) 33.

Giakoumakis E, 'A Riddle Wrapped in a Mystery Inside an Enigma': Equitable Considerations in the Assessment of Damages by Investment Tribunals' in P Merkouris, A Kulick, JM Alvarez-Zarate and M Zenkiewicj (eds), *Custom and its Interpretation in International Investment Law* (CUP 2024) 179.

Goldsmith JL and EA Posner, *Limits of International Law* (OUP 2007).

Grotius H, *The Law of War and Peace* [*De Jure Belli ac Pacis*] (1625).

Hart HLA, *The Concept of Law* (3rd edn, OUP 2012).

Henin PF, '*In Pari Materia* Interpretation' in J Klingler, Y Parkhomenko and C Salonidis (eds), *Between the Lines of the Vienna Convention? Canons and Other Principles of Interpretation in Public International Law* (Wolters Kluwer 2018) 211.

Hollis DB, 'Sources in Interpretation Theories: An Interdependent Relationship' in S Besson and J d' Aspremont (eds), *The Oxford Handbook on the Sources of International Law* (OUP 2017) 422.

Hollis DB, 'The Existential Function of Interpretation in International Law' in A Bianchi, D Peat and M Windsor (eds), *Interpretation in International Law* (OUP 2015) 78.

Kammerhofer J, *International Investment Law and Legal Theory* (CUP 2021).

Klingler J, Y Parkhomenko and C Salonidis (eds), *Between the Lines of the Vienna Convention? Canons and Other Principles of Interpretation in Public International Law* (Wolters Kluwer 2018).

Kohen M, 'Keeping Subsequent Agreements and Practice in Their Right Limits' in G Nolte (ed), *Treaties and Subsequent Practice* (OUP 2013) 34.

Kolb R, *Interprétation et création du droit international: esquisses d' une herméneutique juridique moderne pour le droit international public* (Bruylant 2006).

Krisch N, 'Pluralism' in J d'Aspremont and S Singh (eds), *Concepts for International Law: Contributions to Disciplinary Thought* (Edward Elgar 2019) 691.

le Bouthillier Y and J-F Bonin, 'Article 3 – Convention of 1969' in O Corten and P Klein (eds), *The Vienna Convention on the Law of Treaties: A Commentary* (OUP 2011) 66.

Lekkas S, 'The Uses of the Work of the International Law Commission on State Responsibility in International Investment Arbitration' in P Merkouris, A Kulick, JM Alvarez-Zarate and M Zenkiewicj (eds), *Custom and its Interpretation in International Investment Law* (CUP 2024) 93.

Lijnzaad L and Council of Europe (eds), *The Judge and International Custom / Le juge et la coutume internationale* (Brill 2016).

Marcus Tullius Cicero, *De Officiis*.

Margaritis M, 'Article 559' in K Kerameas, D Kondilis and N Nikas, *Interpretation of the Code of Civil Procedure, Vol 1, Articles 1–590* (Sakkoulas 2000) 1000.

Merkouris P, *Article 31(3)(c) and the Principle of Systemic Integration: Normative Shadows in Plato's Cave* (Brill/Nijhoff 2015).

Merkouris P, 'The Correct Interpretation Premise in International Adjudication' in P Westerman, K Gorobets and A Hadjigeorgiou (eds), *Conceptual (De)Constructions of International Law* (Edward Elgar 2022) 215.

Merkouris P, RA Wessel and IT de Vries-Zou (eds), *The European Union and the Interpretation of Customary International Law* (Asser Institute, CLEER Papers 2024/1) <https://www.asser.nl/media/796897/cleer_024-01_web-final.pdf>.

Mileva N, *A Theory of Interpretation for Customary International Law* (University of Groningen, 2023).

Mileva N, 'The Role of Domestic Courts in the Interpretation of Customary International Law: How can we Learn from Domestic Interpretive Practices?' in P Merkouris, J Kammerhofer and N Arajärvi (eds), *The Theory, Practice and Interpretation of Customary International Law* (CUP 2022) 453.

Mitchell AD and T Voon, 'The Rule of Necessary Implication' in J Klingler, Y Parkhomenko and C Salonidis (eds), *Between the Lines of the Vienna Convention? Canons and Other Principles of Interpretation in Public International Law* (Wolters Kluwer 2018) 331.

Müller F, *Discours de la méthode juridique* (O Jouanjan tr, Presses Universitaires de France 1996).

Murphy S, 'The Relevance of Subsequent Agreement and Subsequent Practice in the Interpretation of Treaties' in G Nolte (ed), *Treaties and Subsequent Practice* (OUP 2013) 82.

Nollkaemper A, *The Practice of International and National Courts and the (De-)fragmentation of International Law* (Hart Publishing 2012).

O'Connell DP, *International Law, Vol 1* (2nd edn, Stevens and Sons 1970).

Orakhelashvili A, *The Interpretation of Acts and Rules in Public International Law* (OUP 2008).

Pazartzis Ph, 'Le rôle de la pratique dans le droit coutumier' in RH Vinaixa (ed), *L'influence des sources sur l'unité et la fragmentation du droit international* (Bruylant 2006) 81.

Polyaenus, *Stratagems.*

Polybius, *Histories.*

Ruiz Fabri H, *Sur quelques aspects de la théorie de la coutume en droit international contemporain* (Thèse soutenue en 1989 à Bordeaux 1).

Ryngaert C, 'Customary International Law Interpretation: The Role of Domestic Courts' in P Merkouris, J Kammerhofer and N Arajärvi (eds), *The Theory, Practice and Interpretation of Customary International Law* (CUP 2022) 481.

Schmalenbach K, 'Article 2' in O Dörr and K Schmalenbach (eds), *Vienna Convention on the Law of Treaties: A Commentary* (2nd edn, Springer 2018) 29.

Schmalenbach K, 'Article 3' in O Dörr and K Schmalenbach (eds), *Vienna Convention on the Law of Treaties: A Commentary* (Springer 2018) 55.

Sorensen R, *A Brief History of the Paradox: Philosophy and the Labyrinths of the Mind* (OUP 2003).

Staubach P, 'The Interpretation of Unwritten International Law by Domestic Judges' in HP Aust and G Nolte (eds), *The Interpretation of International Law by Domestic Courts: Unity, Diversity, Convergence* (OUP 2016) 113.

Sur S, *L'interprétation en droit international public* (LGDJ 1974).

Thirlway H, *International Customary Law and Codification: An Examination of the Continuing Role of Custom in the Present Period of International Law* (Sijthoff 1972).

Thucydides, *The Peloponnesian War.*

Titus Livius (Livy), *Ab Urbe Condita.*

Trachtman JP, 'The Growing Obsolescence of Customary International Law' in CA Bradley (ed), *Custom's Future: International Law in a Changing World* (CUP 2016) 172.

Tzevelekos VP, '*Juris dicere*: Custom as a Matrix, Custom as a Norm, and the Role of Judges and (their) Ideology in Custom Making' in N Rajkovic, TE Aalberts and Th Gammeltoft-Hansen (eds), The Power of Legality: Practices of International Law and their Politics (CUP 2016) 188.

Valerius Maximus, *Valeri Maximi Factorum et Dictorum Memorabilium.*

Villiger M, *Commentary on the 1969 Vienna Convention on the Law of Treaties* (Brill/Nijhoff 2008).

Wolfke K, *Custom in Present International Law* (2nd edn, Brill/Martinus Nijhoff 1993) 116.

Zarbiyev F, 'Les règles d'interprétation de la Convention de Vienne sur le droit des traités: un outil d'harmonisation en droit international?' in C Chappuis et al (eds), *L'harmonisation internationale du droit* (Schulthess 2007) 75.

Articles

Akehurst M, 'Custom as a Source of International Law' (1977) 47 BYIL 1.

Alland D, 'L' interprétation du droit international public' (2013) 362 RdC 1.

Banteka N, 'A Theory of Constructive Interpretation for Customary International Law Identification' (2018) 39/3 MichJIntlL 301.

Barile G, 'Il metodo logico-storico di rilevazione del diritto internazionale non scritto e le sue radici giusnaturalistiche' (1989) 72 Rivista di diritto internazionale 7.

Barile G, 'La rilevazione e l'integrazione del diritto internazionale non scritto e la libertà di apprezzamento del giudice' (1953) 5 Comunicazioni e studi 141.

Barile G, 'La structure de l' ordre juridique international: règles générales et règles conventionnelles' (1978/III) 161 RdC 9.

Bentivoglio LM, 'Per una interpretazione funzionale del diritto internazionale' [1965] Annuario di diritto internazionale 32.

Benvenisti E, 'Reclaiming Democracy: The Strategic Uses of Foreign and International Law by National Courts' (2008) 102 AJIL 241.

Bleckmann A, 'Zur Feststellung und Auslegung von Völkergewohnheitsrecht' (1977) 37 ZaöRV 504.

Blutman L, 'Conceptual Confusion and Methodological Deficiencies: Some Ways that Theories on Customary International Law Fail' (2014) 25(2) EJIL 529.

Bos M, 'The Identification of Custom in International Law' (1982) 25 GYIL 9.

Chasapis Tassinis O, 'Customary International Law: Interpretation from Beginning to End' (2020) 31(1) EJIL 235.

Faye J, 'Copenhagen Interpretation of Quantum Mechanics' (*Stanford Encyclopedia of Philosophy*, 6 December 2019) <https://plato.stanford.edu/entries/qm-copenhagen/>.

Fitzmaurice M, 'The Identification and Character of Treaties and Treaty Obligations Between States in International Law' (2002) 73 BYIL 141.

French D, 'Treaty Interpretation and the Incorporation of Extraneous Legal Rules' (2006) 55 ICLQ 281.

Garner JW, 'Codification of International Law: Part III – Law of Treaties – Appendix 4: Fiore's Draft Code' (1935) 29 AJIL Supp 1212.

Georgopoulos Th, 'Le droit intertemporel et les dispositions conventionelles évolutives – quelle thérapie contre la vieillesse des traités?' (2004) 108/1 RGDIP 123.

Goldstein Sh, 'Bohmian Mechanics' (*Stanford Encyclopedia of Philosophy*, 14 June 2021) <https://plato.stanford.edu/entries/qm-bohm/>.

Haggenmacher P, 'La doctrine des deux éléments du droit coutumier dans la pratique de la Cour internationale' (1986) 90 RGDIP 5.

Hakimi M, 'Making Sense of Customary International Law' (2020) 118/8 MichLRev 1487.

Hart HLA, 'Positivism and the Separation of Law and Morals' (195) 71/4 Harvard Law Review 607.

Helmersen ST, 'Evolutive Treaty Interpretation: Legality, Semantics and Distinctions' (2013) 6 EurJLegStud 127.

Herdegen M, 'Interpretation in International Law' [2013] MPEPIL 723.

Hexner P, 'Interpretation by Public International Organizations of their Basic Instruments' (1959) 53 AJIL 341.

Hyde D and D Raffman, 'Sorites Paradox' (*Stanford Encyclopedia of Philosophy*, 26 March 2018) <https://plato.stanford.edu/entries/sorites-paradox/>.

Jennings R, 'What is International Law and how do we Tell it When we See it?' (1981) 37 Annuaire Suisse de Droit International 59.

Koskenniemi M, 'Introductory Note: International Court of Justice: Order Discontinuing the Proceedings in *Case Concerning Passage Through the Great Belt* (*Finland v Denmark*)' (1993) 32 ILM 101.

Kotzur M, 'Intertemporal Law' [2008] MPEPIL 1433.

Lando M, 'Identification as the Process to Determine the Content of Customary International Law' (2022) 42/4 OJLS 1040–66.

McDade PV, 'The Effect of Article 4 of the Vienna Convention on the Law ofTreaties 1969' (1986) 35 ICLQ 409.

McLachlan C, 'The Principle of Systemic Integration and Article 31(3)(c) of the Vienna Convention' (2005) 54/2 ICLQ 279.

Meijers H, 'How is International Law Made? – The Stages of Growth of International Law and the Use of its Customary Rules' (1978) 9 NYIL 3.

Merkouris P, 'Interpreting the Customary Rules on Interpretation' (2017) 19 ICLR 126.

Merkouris P, 'Principle of Systemic Integration' [2020] MPEiPro 2866.

Merkouris and N Mileva, 'Introduction to the Series: Customary Law Interpretation as a Tool' (2022) 11/1 ESIL Reflections 1, 6 (*ESIL Reflections*, 1 August 2022) <https://esil-sedi.eu/wp-content/uploads/2022/08/ESIL-Reflection-Merkouris-Mileva.pdf>.

Moloo R, 'When Actions Speak Louder Than Words: The Relevance of Subsequent Party Conduct to Treaty Interpretation' (2013) 31/1 BerkJIntlL 39.

Nijman JE and A Nollkaemper, 'Introduction' in JE Nijman and A Nollkaemper (eds), *New Perspectives on the Divide Between National and International Law* (OUP 2007) 1.

Nollkaemper A, 'Decisions of National Courts as Sources of International Law: An Analysis of the Practice of the ICTY' in G Boas and WA Schabas (eds), *International Criminal Developments in the Case Law of the ICTY* (Brill/Martinus Nijhoff 2003) 277.

O' Keefe R, 'The Doctrine of Incorporation Revisited' (2008) 79 BYIL 7.

Prost M, 'Sources and the Hierarchy of International Law: Source Preferences and Scales of Values' in S Besson and J d'Aspremont (eds), *The Oxford Handbook of the Sources of International Law* (OUP 2021) 640.

Qin X, 'Oral International Agreement and China's Relevant Practice' (2005) 4/2 Chinese Journal of International Law 465.

Shany Y, 'National Courts as International Actors: Jurisdictional Implications' (2009) 15 Rivista di diritto pubblico italiano, comunitario e comparato 1 <https://www.federalismi.it/ApplOpenFilePDF.cfm?artid=13810&dpath=document&dfile=29072009111203.pdf&content=National%2Bcourts%2Bas%2Binternational%2Bactors%3A%2Bjurisdictional%2Bimplications%2B%2D%2Bdottrina%2B%2D%2Bdottrina%2B%2D%2B>.

Sur S, 'La créativité du droit international' (2013) 363 RdC 9.

Swart M, 'Judicial Law-Making at the *Ad Hoc* Tribunals: The Creative Use of Sources of International Law and "Adventurous Interpretation"' (2010) 70 Heidelberg Journal of International Law 459.

Talmon S, 'Determining Customary International Law: The ICJ's Methodology between Induction, Deduction and Assertion' (2005) 26(2) EJIL 417.

Tams CJ and A Tzanakopoulos, 'Introduction: Domestic Courts as Agents of Development of International Law' (2013) 26 LJIL 531.

Thirlway H, 'The Law and Procedure of the International Court of Justice 1960–1989: Part One' (1989) 60 BYIL 1.

Treves T, 'Customary International Law' [2006] MPEPIL 1393.

Tzanakopoulos A, 'Domestic Courts in International Law: The International Judicial Function of National Courts' (2011) 34 LoyLAInt'l&CompLRev 133.

Tzevelekos VP, 'The Use of Article 31(3) of the VCLT in the Case Law of the ECtHR: an Effective Anti-Fragmentation Tool or a Selective Loophole for the Reinforcement of Human Rights Teleology?' (2010) 31/3 MichJIntlL 621.

Vierdag EW, 'The Law Governing Treaty Relations Between Parties to the Vienna Convention on the Law of Treaties and States Not Party to the Convention' (1982) 76 AJIL 779.

Widdows K, 'On the Form and Distinctive Nature of International Agreements' (1981) 7(1) Australian YBIL.

International Documents

ICSID, 'ICSID Rules of Procedure for Arbitration Proceedings' (*ICSID*, April 2006) 99 <https://icsid.worldbank.org/sites/default/files/ICSID%20Convention%20English.pdf>.

ILA, 'Final Report of the Committee – Statement of Principles Applicable to the Formation of General Customary International Law' (2000) 69 ILARC 712.

ILA, 'Final Report of the Study Group on Principles on the Engagement of Domestic Courts with International Law: Mapping the Engagement of Domestic Courts with International Law' (*ILA*, 2016) <https://www.ila-hq.org/en_GB/documents/conference-study-group-report-johannesburg-2016>.

ILC, 'Draft Articles on Responsibility of States for Internationally Wrongful Acts with Commentaries' (23 April–1 June and 2 July–10 August 2001) UN Doc A/56/10, reproduced in [2001/II – Part Two] YBILC 31.

ILC, 'Draft Articles on the Law of Treaties with Commentaries' (4 May–19 July 1966) UN Doc A/CN.4/191, reproduced in [1966/II] YBILC 187.

ILC, 'Draft Articles on the Law of Treaties' (24 April–29 June 1962) UN Doc A/5209 reproduced in [1962/II] YBILC 161.

ILC, 'Draft Conclusions on Identification and Legal Consequences of Peremptory Norms of General International Law (*Jus Cogens*), with Commentaries' (2022) UN Doc A/77/10.

ILC, 'Draft Conclusions on Identification of Customary International Law, with Commentaries' (30 April–10 August 2018) UN Doc A/73/10, reproduced in [2018/II – Part Two] YBILC 122.

ILC, 'Draft Conclusions on Subsequent Agreements and Subsequent Practice in Relation to the Interpretation of Treaties, with Commentaries' [2018/II – Part Two] YBILC 16.

ILC, 'Fifth Report on Immunity of State Officials from Foreign Criminal Jurisdiction, by Concepción Escobar Hernández, Special Rapporteur' (14 June 2016) UN Doc A/CN.4/701.

ILC, 'First Report on Formation and Evidence of Customary International Law, by Sir Michael Wood, Special Rapporteur' (17 May 2013) UN Doc A/CN.4/663.

ILC, 'First Report on the Law of Treaties by Sir Humphrey Waldock, Special Rapporteur' (26 March 1962) UN Doc A/CN.4/144 and Add.1 reproduced in [1962/II] YBILC 27.

ILC, 'General Principles of Law: Texts and Titles of Draft Conclusions 1, 2 and 4 Provisionally Adopted by the Drafting Committee' (28 July 2021) UN Doc A/CN.4/L.955.

ILC, 'Guiding Principles Applicable to Unilateral Declarations of States Capable of Creating Legal Obligations with Commentaries Thereto' (1 May–9 June and 3 July–11 August 2006) UN Doc A/61/10 reproduced in [2006/II – Part Two] YBILC 160.

ILC, 'Peremptory Norms of General International Law (*jus cogens*): Text of the Draft Conclusions and Draft Annex Provisionally Adopted by the Drafting Committee on First Reading' (29 May 2019) UN Doc A/CN.4/L.936.

ILC, 'Report of the International Law Commission Covering the Work of its Sixteenth Session' (11 May–24 July 1964) UN Doc A/5809 reproduced in [1964/II] YBILC 173.

ILC, 'Report of the International Law Commission on the Work of its Eighteenth Session' 4 May–19 July 1966) UN Doc A/6309/Rev.l, reproduced in [1966/II] YBILC 172.

ILC, 'Report on Fragmentation of International Law: Difficulties Arising from the Diversification and Expansion of International Law, Finalized by Martti Koskenniemi' (1 May–9 June and 3 July–11 August 2006) UN Doc A/CN.4/L.682.

ILC, 'Report on the Law of Treaties by Mr GG Fitzmaurice' (14 March 1956) UN Doc A/CN.4/101 reproduced in [1956/II] YBILC 104.

ILC, 'Second Report on Identification of Customary International Law, by Michael Wood, Special Rapporteur' (22 May 2014) UN Doc A/CN.4/672.

ILC, 'Sixth Report on the Law of Treaties, by Sir Humphrey Waldock, Special Rapporteur' (11 March–14 June 1966) UN Doc A/CN.4/186 and Add.1–7 reproduced in [1966/II] YBILC 51.

ILC, 'Summary Record of the 668th Meeting' (26 June 1962) UN Doc A/CN.4/SR.668.

ILC, 'Summary Record of the 766th Meeting' (15 July 1964) UN Doc A/CN.4/SR.766.

ILC, 'Summary Record of the 767th Meeting' (16 July 1964) UN Doc A/CN.4/SR.767.

ILC, 'Summary Record of the 866th Meeting' (9 June 1966) UN Doc A/CN.4/SR.866.

ILC, 'Third Report on Peremptory Norms of General International Law (*jus cogens*) by Dire Tladi, Special Rapporteur' (12 February 2018) UN Doc A/CN.4/714.

ILC, 'Third Report on the Law of Treaties by Sir Humphrey Waldock, Special Rapporteur' (3 March, 9 June, 12 June and 7 July 1964) UN Doc A/CN.4/167 and Add.1–3, reproduced in [1964/II] YBILC 5.

Insitut de Droit International, 'IV. Délibérations de l' Institut en séances plénières: Quatriéme Question – De l' interprétation de traités' (1956) 46 AIDI 317.

Institut de Droit International, '7th Commission – Report: Are there Limits to the Dynamic Interpretation of the Constitution and Statutes of International

Organizations by the Internal Organs of such Organizations (with Particular Reference to the UN System)? – Rapporteur M Arsanjani' (*IDI*, 2021) <https://www.idi-iil.org/app/uploads/2021/05/Report-7th-commission-interpretation-statutes-international-organizations-vol-81-yearbook-online-session.pdf>.

Institut de Droit International, '7th Commission – Report: Are there Limits to the Dynamic Interpretation of the Constitution and Statutes of International Organizations by the Internal Organs of such Organizations (with Particular Reference to the UN System)? – Rapporteur M Arsanjani' (2019) 78 AIDI 87.

Institut de Droit International, 'Resolution of 11 August 1975: The Intertemporal Problem in Public International Law' (1975) 56 AIDI 536.

Kenya National Research Team, 'Report on Interpretation of Customary Law in Kenya' (*TRICI-Law*, 2022) <https://tricilawofficial.wordpress.com/wp-content/uploads/2022/02/kenya-final-report_2022.pdf>.

Netherlands, 'ILC Draft Conclusions on the Identification of Customary International Law – Comments and Observations by the Kingdom of the Netherlands' (UN, 2018) <https://legal.un.org/ilc/sessions/70/pdfs/english/icil_netherlands.pdf>.

UN General Assembly, 'Declaration on Principles of International Law concerning Friendly Relations and Cooperation among States in Accordance with the Charter of the United Nations' (24 October 1970) UN Doc A/RES/25/2625.

United Nations Conference on the Law of Treaties, '1st Session–37th Meeting of the Committee of the Whole (COW)' (24 April 1968) UN Doc A/CONF.39/11 203.

United Nations Conference on the Law of Treaties, '1st Session–38th Meeting of the Committee of the Whole (COW)' (25 April 1968) UN Doc A/CONF.39/11 210.

Other

Advisory Committee on Issues of Public International Law (CAVV), 'Advisory Report on the Identification of Customary International Law' (*CAVV*, 2017) <https://www.advisorycommitteeinternationallaw.nl/binaries/cavv-en/documents/advisory-reports/2017/11/01/the-identification-of-customary-international-law/The_identification_of_customary_international_law_CAVV-Advisory-report-29_201711.PDF>.

Branca E, '"Yet, it moves ...": The Dynamic Evolution of State immunity in the "Comfort Women" case' (*EJILTalk!*, 7 April 2021) <https://www.ejiltalk.org/yet-it-moves-the-dynamic-evolution-of-state-immunity-in-the-comfort-women-case/?utm_source=mailpoet&utm_medium=email&utm_campaign=ejil-talk-newsletter-post-title_2>.

Germany, 'On the Application of International Law in Cyberspace – Position Paper' (*Auswärtiges Amt*, March 2021) <https://www.auswaertiges-amt.de/blob/2446304/32e7b2498e10b74fb17204c54665bdf0/on-the-application-of-international-law-in-cyberspace-data.pdf>.

ILC, 'Analytical Guide to the Work of the International Law Commission' (*ILC*, 2023) <https://legal.un.org/ilc/guide/gfra.shtml>.

Lando M, 'Might It Just Work? How To Interpret Customary International Law (Maybe)' (*CIL Dialogues*, 6 March 2023) <https://cil.nus.edu.sg/blogs/might-it-just-work-how-to-interpret-customary-international-law-maybe/>.

Sender O and M Wood, 'The International Court of Justice and Customary International Law: A Reply to Stefan Talmon' (*EJILTalk!*, 30 November 2015) <https://www.ejiltalk.org/the-international-court-of-justice-and-customary-international-law-a-reply-to-stefan-talmon/>.

Talmon S, 'Determining Customary International Law: The ICJ's Methodology and the Idyllic World of the ILC' (*EJILTalk!*, 3 December 2015) <https://www.ejiltalk.org/determining-customary-international-law-the-icjs-methodology-and-the-idyllic-world-of-the-ilc/#more-13882>.

Tladi D, 'Is the International Law Commission Elevating Subsequent Agreements and Subsequent Practice?' (*EJILTalk!*, 30 August 2018) <https://www.ejiltalk.org/is-the-international-law-commission-elevating-subsequent-agreements-and-subsequent-practice/>.

TRICI-Law, 'Draft Guiding Principles on the Interpretation of Customary International Law' (*TRICI-Law*, 2023) <https://tricilawofficial.wordpress.com/draftprinciples/>.

TRICI-Law, 'Draft Guiding Principles on the Interpretation of Customary International Law with Commentaries' (*TRICI-Law*, 2023) <https://tricilawofficial.wordpress.com/draftprinciples/>.

Webb P, 'The Weakest Link of the Troika? The Immunity of Heads of Government in Customary International Law' (*EJILTalk!*, 27 October 2021) <https://www.ejiltalk.org/the-weakest-link-of-the-troika-the-immunity-of-heads-of-government-in-customary-international-law/>.

Wood M and O Sender, 'Between Theory, Practice, and "Interpretation" of Customary International Law' (*CIL Dialogues*, November 2022) <https://cil.nus.edu.sg/blogs/between-theory-practice-and-interpretation-of-customary-international-law/>.

International Case-Law

ICJ

Application of the Convention on the Prevention and Punishment of the Crime of Genocide (*Bosnia and Herzegovina v Serbia and Montenegro*) (Judgment) [2007] ICJ Rep 43.

Application of the Convention on the Prevention and Punishment of the Crime of Genocide (*Croatia v Serbia*) (Merits) [2015] ICJ Rep 3.

Application of the International Convention on the Elimination of All Forms of Racial Discrimination (*Qatar v United Arab Emirates*) (Provisional Measures) [2018] ICJ Rep 406.

Asylum Case (*Colombia/Peru*) [1950] ICJ Rep 266.

Barcelona Traction, Light and Power Company Limited (*New Application: 1962*) (*Second Phase*) (*Belgium v Spain*) (Merits) [1970] ICJ Rep 3.

Case Concerning the Temple of Preah Vihear (*Cambodia v Thailand*) (Merits) [1962] ICJ Rep 6.

Certain Activities carried out by Nicaragua in the Border Area and Construction of a Road in Costa Rica along the San Juan River (*Nicaragua v Costa Rica*) [2015] ICJ Rep 665.

Continental Shelf (*Tunisia v Libyan Arab Jamahiriya*) (Judgment) [182] ICJ Rep 18.

Delimitation of the Maritime Boundary in the Gulf of Maine Area (*Canada v* USA) (Merits) [184] ICJ Rep 246.

Dispute over the Status and Use of the Waters of the Silala (*Chile v. Bolivia*) [2022] ICJ Rep 614.

Fisheries (UK *v Norway*) (Judgment) [1951] ICJ Rep 116.

Gabčíkovo-Nagymaros Project (*HungarylSlovakia*) [1997] ICJ Rep 7.

Interpretation of the Agreement of 25 March 1951 between the WHO *and Egypt* (Advisory Opinion) [1980] ICJ Rep 73.

Jadhav (*India v Pakistan*) (Judgment) [2019] ICJ Rep 418.

Jurisdictional Immunities of the State (*Germany v Italy: Greece intervening*) [2012] ICJ Rep 99.

Kasikili/Sedudu Island (*Botswana/Namibia*) (Judgment) [1999] ICJ Rep 1045.

Maritime Delimitation and Territorial Questions between Qatar and Bahrain (*Qatar v Bahrain*) (Jurisdiction and Admissibility) [1995] ICJ Rep 6.

Maritime Delimitation in the Indian Ocean (*Somalia v Kenya*) (Preliminary Objections) [2017] ICJ Rep 3.

Military and Paramilitary Activities in and against Nicaragua (*Nicaragua v* USA) (Merits) [1986] ICJ Rep 14.

North Sea Continental Shelf (*Germany/Denmark and the Netherlands*) (Judgment) [1969] ICJ Rep 3.

Nuclear Tests (*Australia v France*) (Judgment) [1974] ICJ Rep 253.

Question of the Delimitation of the Continental Shelf between Nicaragua and Colombia beyond 200 nautical miles from the Nicaraguan Coast (*Nicaragua v. Colombia*) ICJ (Judgment of 13 July 2023) <https://www.icj-cij.org/sites/default/files/case-related/154/154-20230713-jud-01-00-en.pdf>.

South-West Africa (*Second Phase*) (*Liberia and Ethiopia v South Africa*) [1966] ICJ Rep 6.

PCIJ

The Mavrommatis Jerusalem Concessions (*Greece v the United Kingdom*) [1925] PCIJ Rep Ser A No 5.

ECtHR

Albert and Le Compte v Belgium, ECtHR, App No 7299/75 (10 February 1983).

Al-Dulimi and Montana Management Inc v Switzerland [GC] ECtHR, App No 5809/08 (21 June 2016).

Al-Saadoon and Mufdhi v UK, ECtHR, App No 61498/08 (2 March 2010).
Bayatyan v Armenia [GC] ECtHR, App No 23459/03 (7 July 2011).
Demir and Baykara v Turkey [GC] ECtHR, App No 34503/97 (12 November 2008).
Feldbrugge v Netherlands, ECtHR, App No 8562/79 (29 May 1986).
Graziani-Weiss v Austria, ECtHR, App No 31950/06 (18 October 2011).
Meftah and others v France [GC] ECtHR, App No 32911/96 (26 July 2002).
National Union of Rail, Maritime and Transport Workers (*RMT*) *v* UK, ECtHR, App No 31045/10 (8 April 2014).
Pini and Others v Romania, ECtHR, App Nos 78028/01 and 78030/01 (22 June 2004).
Soering v UK, ECtHR, App No 14038/88 (7 July 1989).

IACtHR

Claude Reyes and others v Chile (Merits, Reparations and Costs) IACtHR Series C No 151 (19 September 2006).
Ituango Massacres v Colombia (Preliminary Objections, Merits, Reparations and Costs) IACtHR Series C No 148 (1 July 2006).
The Right to Information on Consular Assistance in the Framework of the Guarantees of the Due Process of Law (Advisory Opinion) IACtHR Series A No 16 (1 October 1999).

ICC

Prosecutor v Jean-Pierre Bemba Gombo (Fourth Decision on Victims' Participation of 12 December 2006) ICC Pre-Trial Chamber III, ICC-01/05-01/08-320

ICTY

Prosecutor v Delalić et al (Judgment of 16 November 1998) ICTY Trial Chamber, Case No IT-96-21-T.
Prosecutor v Duško Tadić (Appeal Judgement of 15 July 1999) ICTY Appeals Chamber, Case No IT-94-1-A.
Prosecutor v Enver Hadžihasanović, Mehmed Alagić and Amir Kubura (Decision on Interlocutory Appeal Challenging Jurisdiction in Relation to Command Responsibility of 16 July 2003) ICTY Appeals Chamber, Case No IT-01-47-AR72.
Prosecutor v Naser Orić (Judgment of 3 July 2008) ICTY Appeals Chamber, Case No IT-03-68-A.

CJEU

Case C-284/16 – Slowakische Republik v Achmea BV (6 March 2018) CJEU [GC] ECLI:EU:C:2018:158.

WTO DSB

European Communities – Customs Classification of Frozen Boneless Chicken Cuts – Appellate Body Report (27 September 2005) WT/DS269/AB/R and WT/DS286/AB/R [2005/XIX] DSR 9157.

European Communities – Measures Affecting the Approval and Marketing of Biotech Products – Report of the Panel (21 November 2006) WT/DS291/R 847, WT/DS292/R and WT/DS293/R [2006/III] DSR 847.

Arbitration

AS PNB Banka and others v Latvia (Decision on the intra-EU objection of 14 May 2021) ICSID Case No ARB/17/47.

ATA Construction, Industrial and Trading Company v the Hashemite Kingdom of Jordan (Award of 18 May 2010) ICSID Case No ARB/08/2.

BayWa re renewable energy GmbH and BayWa re Asset Holding GmbH v Spain (Award of 25 January 2021) ICSID Case No ARB/15/16.

Case Concerning a Boundary Dispute between Argentina and Chile Concerning the Frontier Line between Boundary Post 62 and Mount Fitzroy (Argentina v Chile) (1994) 22 UNRIAA 3.

Case Concerning the Air Service Agreement of 27 March (USA *v France*) (1978) 18 UNRIAA 417.

Crystallex v Venezuela (Award of 4 April 2016) ICSID Case No ARB(AF)/11/2.

Devas v India (Decision on Jurisdiction and Merits of 25 July 2016) PCA Case No 2013–09.

EDF International SA, SAUR International SA and Leon Participaciones Argentinas SA v Argentine Republic (Award of 11 June 2012), ICSID Case No ARB/03/23.

EDF International SA, SAUR International SA and Leon Participaciones Argentinas SA v Argentine Republic (Annulment Decision of 5 February 2016) ICSID Case No ARB/03/23.

Mondev International Ltd v USA, (Award of 11 October 2002) ICSID Case No ARB(AF)/99/2.

Quiborax v Bolivia (Award of 16 September 2015) ICSID Case No ARB/06/2.

Silver Ridge Power BV v Italy (Award of 26 February 2021) ICSID Case No ARB/15/37.

Strabag SE and others v Poland (Partial Award on Jurisdiction of 4 March 2020) ICSID Case No ADHOC/15/1.

Tulip v Turkey (Award of 10 March 2014) ICSID Case No ARB/11/28.

Tulip v Turkey (Decision on Annulment of 30 December 2015) ICSID Case No ARB/11/28.

Vattenfall AB and Others v Germany (Decision on the *Achmea* Issue of 31 August 2018) ICSID Case No ARB/12/12.

Treaties

1907 Hague Convention (IV) Hague Convention (IV) Respecting the Laws and Customs of War on Land with Annex of Regulations (adopted 18 October 1907, entered into force 26 January 1910) 36 Stat 2277.

1958 Convention on the High Seas (adopted 29 April 1958, entered into force 30 September 1962) 450 UNTS 11.

1969 Vienna Convention on the Law of Treaties (adopted 23 May 1969, entered into force 27 January 1980) 1155 UNTS 331.

1982 United Nations Convention on the Law of the Sea (adopted 10 December 1982; entered into force 16 November 1994) 1833 UNTS 3.

1991 Agreement on Encouragement and Reciprocal Protection of Investments between the Kingdom of the Netherlands and the Czech and Slovak Federal Republic (adopted 29 April 1991, entered into force 1 October 1992) <https://jusmundi.com/en/document/treaty/en-agreement-on-encouragement-and-reciprocal-protection-of-investments-between-the-kingdom-of-the-netherlands-and-the-czech-and-slovak-federal-republic-netherlands-slovakia-bit-1991-monday-29th-april-1991>.

1992 Convention on Biological Diversity (adopted 5 June 1992, entered into force 29 December 1993) 1760 UNTS 79.

1994 Agreement on the Application of Sanitary and Phytosanitary Measures (SPS Agreement) (adopted 15 April 1994, entered into force 1 January 1995) 1867 UNTS 493.

1994 Energy Charter Treaty (adopted 17 December 1994, entered into force 16 April 1998) 2080 UNTS 100.

1998 Rome Statute of the International Criminal Court (adopted 17 July 1998, entered into force 1 July 2002) 2187 UNTS 3.

2000 Cartagena Protocol on Biosafety to the Convention on Biological Diversity (adopted 29 January 2000, entered into force 11 September 2003) 2226 UNTS 208.

Domestic Case-Law

A v Swiss Federal Public Prosecutor (25 July 2012) Swiss Federal Criminal Court, BB.2011.140.

Attorney-General v Zaoui and Inspector-General of Intelligence and Security and Human Rights Commission (intervening) (21 June 2005) Supreme Court of New Zealand [2005] NZSC 38.

Aziz v Aziz [2008] 2 All ER 501.

Benkharbouche v Embassy of the Republic of Sudan [2019] AC 777.

Case No 2016 Ga-Hap 505092 (8 January 2021) Central District Court of Seoul [3.C.3.6–3.C.3.7] <https://womenandwar.net/resources-eng/?q=YToxOntzOjEyOiJrZXl3b3JkX3R5cGUiO3M6MzoiYWxsIjt9&bmode=view&idx=18323479&t=board> (unofficial translation by Woohee Kim, The Korean Council for Justice and Remembrance for the Issues of Military Sexual Slavery by Japan).

Edwards v Attorney-General for Canada (18 October 1929) Judicial Committee of the Imperial Privy Council [1930] AC 124.

Ferrini v Germany (Appeal Decision of 11 March 2004) Supreme Court of Cassation of Italy, Case No 5044/04.

Former Consular Employee at the Consulate General of Croatia in Stuttgart v Croatia (Second Instance Order of 23 October 2014) Higher Regional Court of Stuttgart, Case No 5 U 52/14, ILDC 2428 (DE 2014).

Harb v Asic [2014] | WLR 4437.

Her Majesty the Queen in Right of Canada v Edelson and others (3 June 1997) Supreme Court of Israel PLA 7092/94, 51(1) PD 625.

Institute of Cetacean Research v Sea Shepherd Conservation Society, 153 F.Supp.3d 1291 (WD Wash 2015).

Institute of Cetacean Research v Sea Shepherd Conservation Society, 725 F.3d 940 (9th Cir 2013).

Jones v Ministry of the Interior of the Kingdom of Saudi Arabia (Secretary of State for Constitutional Affairs intervening) [2007] 1 AC 270.

Jones v Ministry of the Interior of the Kingdom of Saudi Arabia (Secretary of State for Constitutional Affairs intervening) [2007] 1 AC 270.

Judgment 4/2005 (21 April 2005) Areios Pagos, Greece, ΟΛ.ΑΠ 4/2005.

Judgment 7/2006 (23 February 2006) Areios Pagos, Greece, ΟΛ.ΑΠ 7/2006.

Katet Nchoe and another v Republic of Kenya (11 February 2011) High Court of Kenya [2011] eKLR <http://kenyalaw.org/caselaw/cases/view/74018/>.

Martha Wanjiru Kimata and another v Dorcas Wanjiru and another (24 February 2015) High Court of Kenya [2015] eKLR, Civil Appeal No 94 of 2014 <http://kenyalaw.org/caselaw/cases/view/106319/>.

Mighell v Sultan of Johore [1894] | QB 149.

Public Committee against Torture in Israel and Palestinian Society for the Protection of Human Rights and the Environment v Israel and others (13 December 2006) Supreme Court of Israel, HCJ 769/02.

R (Freedom and Justice Party) v Secretary of State for Foreign and Commonwealth Affairs [2019] 2 WLR 578.

R v Amkeyo [1917] EAPLR 14.

R v Bow Street Metropolitan Stipendiary Magistrate ex parte Pinochet Ugarte (No 3) [2000] 1 AC 147.

Re Al M (Immunities) (19 March 2021) High Court of Justice [2021] EWHC 660 (Fam).

Re Al M (Permission to Appeal) (9 June 2021) Court of Appeal [2021] EWCA Civ 890.

Sentenza No 238/2014 (22 October 2014) Italian Constitutional Court <https://www.cortecostituzionale.it/documenti/download/doc/recent_judgments/S238_2013_en.pdf>.

SRYYY *v Minister for Immigration and Multicultural and Indigenous Affairs* (17 March 2005) Federal Court of Australia [2005] FCAFC 42.

The Queen v Alqudsi (Motion to Quash Indictment and Summons for Declaratory Relief of 27 August 2015) Supreme Court of New South Wales, Australia [2015] NSWSC 1222.

Domestic Legislation

Constitution of Greece (2008 rev) <https://www.hellenicparliament.gr/UserFiles/f3c70a23-7696-49db-9148-f24dce6a27c8/001-156%20aggliko.pdf>.

Constitution of Kenya (2010 amendment) <http://www.parliament.go.ke/sites/default/files/2023-03/The_Constitution_of_Kenya_2010.pdf>.

Constitution of the Italian Republic (2020 amendment) <https://www.senato.it/documenti/repository/istituzione/costituzione_inglese.pdf>.

Greek Code of Civil Procedure, ΦΕΚ A 182 19851024.

Judicature Act (2012 rev edn) <http://kenyalaw.org/kl/fileadmin/pdfdownloads/Acts/JudicatureAct_Cap8.pdf>.

State Immunity Act (1978) <https://www.legislation.gov.uk/ukpga/1978/33>.

www.ingramcontent.com/pod-product-compliance
Lightning Source LLC
Chambersburg PA
CBHW071354230926
51846CB00002B/553